# About this Book

The digital camera has revolutionized photography, especially for the home user. Now anyone can edit, enhance and print their own photographs at home, present them in a slide show or use the Internet to share them with friends anywhere in the world. Digital cameras have a "point and click" automatic mode so you don't need to worry about manual settings such as exposure, etc., although these are still available if you want to use them.

This book starts by discussing various types of camera, from the cheapest Compact camera through to the more expensive DSLR models. The memory card at the centre of all digital cameras is described, as well as the necessary computing equipment. Downloading the essential Windows Live Photo Gallery software, available free from the Internet, is also described.

The deleting of unwanted images and the selection of the images you wish to import to your computer are then discussed. Various programs are available within Microsoft Windows for viewing images on a computer, singly and in slide shows and these are described. Then follows a detailed description of the easy to use organising, viewing and editing facilities of the Windows Live Photo Gallery. The Windows Paint program is also discussed.

A later chapter describes how photos can be printed at home or at one of the many commercial printing companies. Sending of photos around the world using e-mail or photo sharing Web sites is also described. The final chapter shows how the Windows Explorer program can be used to organise and manage your photos in folders and create secure backup copies on a CD.

Windows XP users may wish to read the brief notes at the end of the book, which describe some slight differences between XP and the two latest versions, Windows Vista and Windows 7.

By the same author as the best-selling and highly acclaimed "Computing for the Older Generation" (BP601) and "Getting Started in Computing for the Older Generation — Windows 7 Edition" (BP717).

## About the Author

Jim Gatenby trained as a Chartered Mechanical Engineer and initially worked at Rolls-Royce Ltd using computers in the analysis of jet engine performance. He obtained a Master of Philosophy degree in Mathematical Education by research at Loughborough University of Technology and taught mathematics and computing in school for many years before becoming a full-time author. His most recent teaching posts included Head of Computer Studies and Information Technology Coordinator. The author has written over thirty books in the field of educational computing, including many of the titles in the highly successful Older Generation series from Bernard Babani (publishing) Ltd.

## Trademarks

Microsoft, Windows, Windows XP, Windows Vista, Windows 7, Windows Live Photo Gallery, Windows Photo Viewer, Windows Mail, Internet Explorer, Paint and Hotmail are either trademarks or registered trademarks of Microsoft Corporation. All other brand and product names used in this book are recognized as trademarks or registered trademarks of their respective companies.

## Acknowledgements

As usual I would like to thank my wife Jill for her continued support during the preparation of this book.

# Computing and Digital Photography for the Older Generation

Jim Gatenby

BERNARD BABANI (publishing) LTD
The Grampians
Shepherds Bush Road
London W6 7NF
England

www.babanibooks.com

## Please Note

Although every care has been taken with the production of this book to ensure that all information is correct at the time of writing and that any projects, designs, modifications and/or programs, etc., contained herewith, operate in a correct and safe manner and also that any components specified are normally available in Great Britain, the Publishers and Author do not accept responsibility in any way for the failure (including fault in design) of any project, design, modification or program to work correctly or to cause damage to any equipment that it may be connected to or used in conjunction with, or in respect of any other damage or injury that may be so caused, nor do the Publishers accept responsibility in any way for the failure to obtain specified components.

Notice is also given that if equipment that is still under warranty is modified in any way or used or connected with home-built equipment then that warranty may be void.

First Published – November 2011

British Library Cataloguing in Publication Data:

A catalogue record for this book is available from the British Library

ISBN 978-0-85934-729-7

Cover Design by Gregor Arthur

Printed and bound in Great Britain for Bernard Babani (publishing) Ltd

# Contents

**3**

---

## Connecting the Memory Card 25
## to a Computer

**4**

---

## Copying Photographs and Videos 37
## to a Computer

## 10

## Managing Photos in Windows Explorer   105

## Appendix: Notes for Users of Windows XP   115

## Index                                                                   117

## Conventions Used in this Book

Words which appear on the screen in menus, etc., are shown in the text in bold, for example, **Print Preview**.

Certain words appear on the screen using the American spelling, such as **Disk Cleanup** for example. These are used where the text refers to words displayed on the screen.

## Mouse Operation

Throughout this book, the following terms are used to describe the operation of the mouse:

### Click

A single press of the left-hand mouse button.

### Double-click

Two presses of the left-hand mouse button, in rapid succession.

### Right-click

A single press of the right-hand mouse button. Used to display context-sensitive menus.

### Drag and Drop

To transfer a file or folder to a new folder or disc drive, select the file or folder and, while keeping the left-hand button held down, drag the object until it is over the destination folder or disc drive, which will appear highlighted. Release the mouse button to complete the process. If you drag with the right button held down, a menu appears allowing you to either **Copy** or **Move** the object. **Move** deletes it from its original location.

## Further Reading

If you enjoy reading this book and find it helpful, you may be interested in a companion book by the same author, **An Introduction to the Internet for the Older Generation (BP711)** from Bernard Babani (publishing) Ltd and available from all good bookshops.

# Getting Started

## Advantages of Digital Photography

Recent years have seen a huge rise in the popularity of the digital camera, together with the widespread use of home computers. As a result, millions of people now enjoy producing their own good quality prints, without specialist knowledge or expensive photographic equipment. This is particularly valuable for older people (including myself) who may have more time to record special family occasions or take photographs of holidays, landscapes or memorable gardens, for example. Digital photography using a computer has many advantages compared with the traditional film camera, including the following:

- Digital photographs are cheaper and can be printed immediately within the comfort of your own home, using an inexpensive inkjet photo printer.

- Photographs can be checked before printing and any unwanted images easily deleted from the camera.

- Images can be edited on the computer to improve the quality or may be "cropped" to remove surplus material.

- You can use the Internet to share your photos with friends and family anywhere in the world. This includes attaching photos to e-mails, or posting to one of the photo-sharing Web sites such as Flickr or Facebook.

- Using a computer, your photos can be arranged in albums, viewed as a slide show or displayed on a screen via a projector, to illustrate a talk or discussion.

- Many digital cameras can also make video recordings.

- All of the work in this book can be done using the Windows Live Photo Gallery software, available free for users of Microsoft Windows XP, Vista and Windows 7.

# Types of Digital Camera
## The Compact Camera

A few years ago the cheapest digital cameras cost several hundred pounds, putting them out of reach of many people. Nowadays some very capable digital cameras can be obtained for under £50; as shown below on the right these small devices fit easily into the palm of your hand and are known as Compact cameras. Despite their price they are more than capable of producing  good quality photographs quickly and easily. They are also easy to use, with automatic settings allowing you to simply "point and click" — although manual settings are also available.

## The DSLR Camera

By spending upwards of £300 you could buy a Digital Single-Lens Reflex camera, more like those used by professionals. The DSLR camera has interchangeable lenses for different purposes, such as long-distance wildlife photos or close-ups of flowers.The DSLR (and its predecessor the SLR film camera) can take lots of images repeatedly at high speed and displays on the screen or viewfinder an exact preview of the finished photograph  —  not always true with the Compact camera.

**DSLR**          **Compact Camera**

## The Bridge Camera

There is a range of cameras of increasing sophistication between the two extremes of the cheapest Compact camera and the DSLR just discussed. These include the Advanced Compact, the Compact System, and the Bridge camera. These cameras have extra zoom and other advanced features; the Compact System also has interchangeable lenses like the DSLR. The Bridge camera has one fixed lens which may have 20x to 30x zoom capability. Zoom enables the camera to photograph distant objects and is discussed in more detail in the next chapter. Typical prices for these mid-range cameras are £150-£400.

Shown below is an Olympus SP800 Bridge camera. At the time of writing this popular camera was available on the Internet from various suppliers at prices ranging from £210-£250. The advertised specification included "14MP, 30x Wide Optical Zoom, 3.0 inch LCD". The terms MP and Optical Zoom are explained in the next chapter. 3.0 inch LCD refers to the size of the small screen on the back of the camera used to set up a shot, view and, if necessary delete, saved photographs. The screen also displays the menus used to set up and operate the camera.

**Bridge Camera**

## Memory Cards

One of the main features of the digital camera which distinguishes it from the traditional film camera is the use of a removable *memory card* on which hundreds or even thousands of photographs can be stored. It is a type of *flash memory*, on which data can be repeatedly written, deleted and rewritten electronically. The memory card may be included with the camera or may have to be bought separately. There are several types of memory card, such as the popular SanDisk SD card shown on the right.

There are numerous quick and easy ways to copy the images from the memory card to a computer, as discussed later. Then they can be saved on the computer's hard disc or stored on a CD to create a permanent, virtually indestructible archive.

Memory cards can be bought from many high street stores, with capacities ranging from 1GB (gigabyte) up to 16GB or even 32GB. A card of 2GB costing about £4 or one of 8GB costing £8 upwards (depending on the specification) should be more than adequate although you may also wish to have a few spare cards.

As the cards can be used repeatedly by deleting images and recording new ones, backup copies of photos should be made on your computer's hard disc and better still on a CD-R or DVD-R.

Once stored in the computer the images can be improved by editing, printed on photo paper or shared with other people all over the world by sending across the Internet. All of these methods are discussed in detail later in this book.

As well as the memory card, a digital camera may also have some internal memory on which a few photos can be stored.

**Jargon Note: A typical photo might be 3MB (3Megabytes) in size. 1GB (Gigabyte) is a thousand Megabytes. So an 8GB card could quite easily hold over 2000 photographs.**

# Batteries

Batteries are a major consideration with digital cameras, especially for long trips or holidays away from home. Power is used by the digital camera to illuminate the small screen on the back of the camera, to power the zoom lens and to transfer photos to a computer, as discussed shortly.

Some cheaper digital cameras are supplied with standard AA batteries obtainable anywhere, but these are very quickly exhausted. To replace them you can buy some *rechargeable* AA batteries such as NiCad or NiMH. It's worth having a spare set and obviously a battery charger, costing a few pounds.

Rechargeable *lithium ion* (or *Li-ion*) batteries as shown on the right are now standard on many cameras because of their longer life. The lithium ion battery uses a special charger, as shown below. The charger is normally included with a new camera.

Apart from batteries, some digital cameras, such as the Olympus range, also have an optional *mains adaptor*. This is useful when "downloading" images from your camera to a computer, a process heavy on battery power.

## USB Cable

The package should include a cable to connect the camera to one of the USB ports on the computer, to enable images to be transferred and saved on the computer, as discussed shortly. Most modern computers have several of the small rectangular USB ports (like the two shown on the right) which are used to connect various peripheral devices such as printers and flash drives. If you don't have a vacant USB port, you can buy a cheap adaptor containing several additional ports.

# The Computer

Any computer made in the last few years will be quite capable of managing and printing your digital photographs. The two main types of computer are the IBM PC compatible and the Apple range, including the MacBook and the iPad. The PC is the most commonly used computer throughout the world and technical support and spares and accessories are readily available everywhere. Apple products are renowned for their quality and innovative features but they are relatively expensive. This book has been produced using a PC computer and is particularly suitable for users of the Microsoft Windows XP, Vista and Windows 7 operating systems.

### Laptop or Desktop

Nowadays the small laptop computer has the power, and performance equivalent to much larger desktop machines. The laptop is a good choice for digital photography work. With its 15in diagonal screen you can display your photographs clearly; the portability means you can work on photographs anywhere in your home. This portability also means you can take the laptop away from home, perhaps to show photographs to friends or illustrate a talk using a projector. A capable laptop can now be bought for under £300; you might also consider the smaller and cheaper Netbook computer with a typical screen size of 10 inches (measured diagonally). Modern laptops have the USB ports needed to connect a camera or card reader. Some laptops also  have a built-in card reader to transfer photographs directly, without connecting the camera to the computer.

Methods of copying photographs from the camera to the computer are discussed in detail in Chapter 4.

# The Printer

For the home user printing digital photographs, there are lots of inexpensive inkjet printers (some of which are called "photo" printers) for as little as £50 upwards. Even the cheaper printers can produce good quality prints, especially if you use special glossy photo paper. The Achilles heal with some inkjet printers is that a set of genuine ink cartridges can cost nearly as much as the printer itself. It's worth shopping around on the Internet for replacement cartridges; also consider "compatible" products rather than "genuine" ones from the printer manufacturer. You can also buy refill kits to replenish empty cartridges.

The latest multi-function printers (often shortened to MFP) can also act as photo-copiers and scanners. Shown on the right is a multi-function inkjet printer from Brother and there are competing models from all of the major printer manufacturers such as Hewlett Packard (HP), Canon, Epson and Lexmark, etc. If you have a wireless network you can print from anywhere in your home and in addition special *wireless printers*  don't even need to be attached by a cable to a computer.

### Scanning a Photographic Print

The scanning facility is useful if you have a photograph on paper which you want to edit, enhance or send across the Internet, etc. The scanner "digitises" the photograph, i.e. converts it into a digital photograph consisting of millions of binary digits (0s and 1s) suitable for input to the computer. The new digital photograph is then saved as a file in the computer where it can be edited and managed in various ways as described throughout this book. You can also buy dedicated scanners which are not part of a printer.

## Software for Managing Digital Photographs

A new digital camera usually has a CD or DVD containing software for managing photographs. Or you can buy software such as Adobe Photoshop Elements, the home user version of Adobe Photoshop, used by professionals in photography and publishing. Programs like this have tools allowing you, for example, to enhance an image or modify it in various ways.

However, Microsoft provides its own free photographic software for use with their Windows operating systems. This book features the Windows Live Photo Gallery, shown below, which contains everything you need to get the most out of your photos. The Photo Gallery is available free for users of Windows XP, Vista and Windows 7 and is discussed in detail later in this book. Other Windows software useful for digital photography includes Windows Paint and Windows Photo Viewer discussed later.

## Functions of Software for Managing Photos

Some of the main functions of the software needed to manage and process photographs in a computer are listed below. These tasks are described in the remainder of this book, using the software provided with, or freely available for, Microsoft Windows XP, Vista and Windows 7.

- Manage the selection and transfer of photographic images from the camera to the computer.

- Permanently save the images as files on the computer, in various formats for different purposes.

- Organise the photographs into libraries, albums or folders so that they can easily be retrieved.

- Edit the images to enhance the quality, e.g. by adjusting the brightness or contrast or by removing undesirable effects such as "red eye".

- Further edit the images by "cropping" to remove unwanted background material, objects or people.

- Display photographs individually on the screen or as a slide show.

- Display movies created using a digital camera, including sound and video.

- Output images from the computer to various destinations, such as a photo printer, an e-mail message or a photo-sharing Web site.

- Copy, i.e. back up, images to a CD/DVD to make a secure archive of important or valuable photographs.

- Reduce the size of the file representing the image saved on disc, so that it can be sent more easily as an e-mail attachment or posted to a Web site.

## Downloading Windows Live Photo Gallery

The Photo Gallery is part of a suite of programs known as Windows Live Essentials. If it's already installed on your computer the program will appear in the **Start/All Programs** menu, as shown on the

right. Otherwise, you can download a free copy of the Windows Live Photo Gallery after entering the following into the Address Bar of a Web browser program such as Internet Explorer:

### http://explore.live.com

Allow the cursor to hover over the word **Essentials**, then from the resulting drop-down menu click **Great photos: Photo Gallery**. Next click the **Download now** button shown above and make sure the **Photo Gallery** is included in the download. After a few minutes, you will be asked to restart the computer to complete the process. **Windows Live Photo Gallery** should now appear in the **Start/All Programs** menu as shown at the top right above.

A separate version of the Photo Gallery for Windows XP can be downloaded from this Web site.

# The Digital Camera

## Introduction

The digital camera is very easy to use as a "point and click" device. However, there are still a few control dials and buttons you need to be familiar with to start taking photographs. Shown below is the front view of a typical Compact camera.

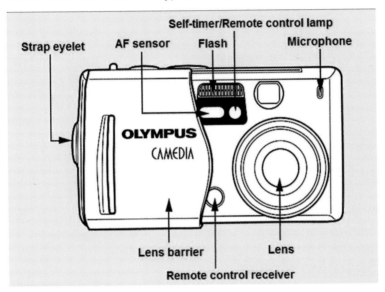

The above camera is switched on and off by moving the Lens barrier; alternatively a separate on/off switch is often located on the top of a camera. If the camera is not used for a few minutes it may go into standby mode to save power. You can usually exit standby mode by switching the camera back on or by gently pressing the shutter button. The shutter button is used to take photos and is shown on the diagram on the next page.

The flash unit can be set to auto mode so that extra light is automatically supplied whenever necessary.

The top view of a Compact camera shown below includes some of the most important controls on a digital camera. The shutter button is used for taking a photograph. On the right is the zoom lever which allows you to photograph distant objects by moving the lens outwards. This is known as *optical zoom* and is discussed in more detail shortly. On some cameras the zoom lever and the shutter button are combined into a single unit.

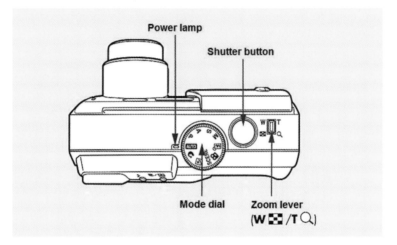

In the diagram above, the lever position T represents the Telephoto or "zoom in" setting used to capture distant objects. W represents the Wide angle or "zoom out" setting.

## Shooting Modes

You set the Mode dial shown above according to the type of photograph being taken. For example, there is a fully automatic mode for beginners, a macro mode for taking close-ups of flowers, etc., and other modes for portraits and scenes such as landscapes, sporting shots and video. The playback mode is used to view the photos and videos you've already captured and saved on your memory card. These are displayed on the small LCD monitor on the back of the camera, as shown at the top of the next page. These screens are typically about 3 inches wide.

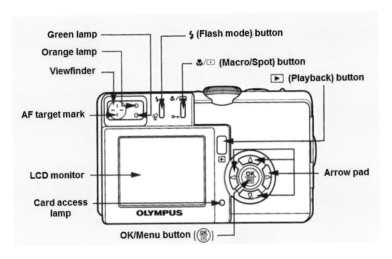

Unlike the traditional film camera, the photos you take on a digital camera are immediately viewable on the monitor in playback mode. So you can review what you've taken and, if necessary, try to take some better ones. Any images you don't want can easily be deleted using one of the buttons on the back of the camera, usually marked with an icon representing a rubbish bin. A memory card can be used repeatedly to save and if necessary delete photographs. In playback mode you can use the zoom lever to enlarge the image on the back of the camera. If you zoom out as far as possible the monitor displays a gallery of miniature images of the latest photos saved on the card.

The circular arrow pad shown above and on the right is used to scroll through the images as you are playing them back. It is also used to display the menus which control the settings on the camera. The arrow buttons 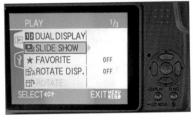 shown enable movement around the menu options and the central OK button allows an option to be selected.

# Resolution

This refers to the number of *small pixels* or *picture elements* (small coloured squares) used to make up a photograph. Higher resolution images can be enlarged and still retain their clarity; low resolution images become "chunky" when enlarged.

The resolution is determined by a device in the camera known as the *CCD (charge coupled device)*. This, together with the memory, replaces the film in the conventional camera. The CCD is an *image sensor* which converts light from the subject of the photograph into an image stored on the memory card.

A few years ago, a mid-range camera costing about £200 would typically have a maximum resolution of 1600 x 1200 pixels, or about 2 million pixels (2MP) (usually stated as 2 *megapixels*). Nowadays a similarly priced mid-range camera might have a resolution of 4288 x 3216 pixels or about 14 megapixels (14MP).

You can change the resolution using the menus on a digital camera. The extracts from the Windows Explorer on the next page show the details of two photographs immediately after copying from a camera's memory card to a hard disc. The top image was taken with the camera set at its maximum 14MP or 4288 x 3216 pixels. The lower image was taken with the camera set at 2MP or 1600 x 1200. As discussed later, you can reduce the resolution of a stored photograph using software such as Windows Live Photo Gallery. The quality of low resolution photographs may be quite acceptable for viewing on  the Internet or with an e-mail. However, high capacity memory cards are now quite cheap, so the storage space occupied by high resolution images is no longer such a big issue. The problem with high resolution images is that at 3.00MB (megabytes) or more they may be too big to send in an e-mail or to post on a Web site.

**If you are not familiar with bits, bytes, megabytes, pixels, etc., please see the notes on page 24.**

Item type: JPEG Image
Date taken: 26/06/2011 10:41 AM
Rating: Unrated
Dimensions: 4288 x 3216
Size: 3.00 MB
Title: OLYMPUS DIGITAL CAMERA

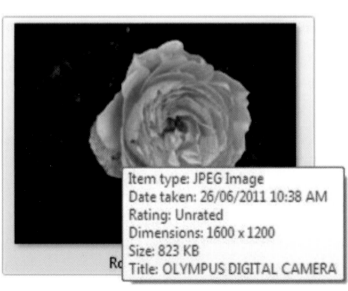

Item type: JPEG Image
Date taken: 26/06/2011 10:38 AM
Rating: Unrated
Dimensions: 1600 x 1200
Size: 823 KB
Title: OLYMPUS DIGITAL CAMERA

# Key Points: Resolution

- Resolution is the number of pixels or dots used to make up an image. Currently 14 megapixels (14MP) is typical.

- Compared with lower resolution images, higher resolution photos can be enlarged to a greater size, without losing quality or becoming "pixellated" i.e. showing the small coloured squares or pixels which make up the image.

- Images are saved as JPEG files (Joint Photographic Experts Group) on the camera's memory card and on the computer. JPEG is a very common format used to store digital photographs.

- A high resolution image (14MP, say) can easily have a file size of 3MB (megabytes). This is a measure of the space occupied on the memory card or hard disc, etc.

- A low resolution image (2MP, say) might have a file size of about 800KB. (1MB = 1024KB).

- A 4GB (gigabyte) memory card can hold about 1200 high resolution images or several thousand low resolution images. (1GB = 1024MB).

- High resolution images may be too big or too slow to send by e-mail or to post to Web sites. The camera can be set to take photographs at a lower resolution using the dials, buttons and menus on the back of the camera.

- High resolution images already transferred from a camera and saved on a computer can be reduced in size prior to e-mailing using software such as Windows Live Photo Gallery, discussed in detail later in this book.

- Low resolution images (2MP say) may be quite all right for small size prints (up to about 7" x 5") and for sending in e-mails or on Web sites.

# Optical Zoom

This is the ability of a camera to take close-up pictures of a distant object. In a compact camera this is achieved by using a small lever to move the lens in and out. In a DSLR camera, zoom is altered by fitting different lenses and by rotating the lens to produce outward or inward movement.

The cheapest compact cameras have an optical zoom of 3x compared with 20x or 30x upwards in more expensive models.

You don't need to understand how these figures are calculated in order to choose a digital camera; however, they are a measure of the change in the *focal length* of the camera between extremes of the zoom movement. The focal length is the distance between the centre of the lens and a *focal point* on the camera. So a camera with a focal length of 35mm (unextended) and a focal length of 105mm (extended) would have an optical zoom of 3x.

The extreme positions of the zoom lever are marked on the camera as T (telephoto or zoom in) and W (wide angle or zoom out) as shown on the right. The T position gives a narrow view of a  distant object.; the W position emphasises the foreground and makes the background seem more distant.

# Digital Zoom

Not to be confused with optical zoom, this is often criticised by experts because it refers to the camera using its own built-in software to enlarge the centre of an image, unlike optical zoom which takes a genuine close-up shot by physically moving the lens. Digital zoom can be switched off on many cameras and some experts recommend this. They prefer to wait until the image has been transferred to a computer. Then the image can be cropped to leave only the required area. This can then be enlarged using the computer's software, such as the Windows Live Photo Gallery, discussed later in this book.

# The Battery and Memory Card

These two essential components are often housed in the same compartment. Access is gained by sliding away a small metal cover at the bottom of the camera.

In the image shown on the right, the metal cover has been slid open and raised. The blue object is the bottom edge of the memory card. The silver and black lithium ion  battery is shown to the right, held in place by an orange plastic lever. The black circle in the upper centre is a threaded hole to allow a tripod to be fitted to the camera

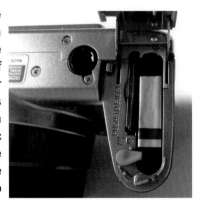

**Removing and Replacing a Memory Card**

To remove the memory card gently press the card towards the inside of the camera. The card springs out enough for you to withdraw it with your fingers.

To replace a memory card, gently slide it into position until it clicks into place. Do not apply undue force — the card only fits one way and should slip easily into place.

Although memory cards are now relatively cheap and can each store hundreds or thousands of photographs, you'll probably want to have separate cards for different purposes or to keep one or two spares. An 8GB card capable of storing thousands of images can currently be bought for under £8 (plus postage) if you shop around the Internet.

It's a good idea to back up important photos to a secure medium such as a CD-R/DVD-R, since images can easily be overwritten or deleted from the memory card (or from a computer's hard disc drive). Backing up photos in a secure archive is discussed later.

**Safeguarding Images on a Memory Card**

A small tab on the side of an SD card can be slid down to lock the card; with the tab in the locked position, no more images can be saved on the card and existing ones can't be deleted. On the card shown on the right, the locking tab is about a third of the way down the left-hand edge, to the left of the name **SanDisk**. Obviously the tab will  need to be moved to the unlocked position to start using it again to save images in a camera .

**Removing and Replacing a Battery**

In some cameras the battery must be removed from the camera for charging. In others, you charge the battery by simply connecting the complete camera to a power point or to a computer, using special cables provided with the camera.

You need to make sure the battery is fully charged before setting off on a trip or on holiday. It's also a good idea to have at least one spare battery in reserve. It's recommended that a battery is discharged and recharged at regular intervals.

To remove the battery, slide away the thin metal cover, then gently push aside the small plastic lever or button. The battery should then spring out sufficiently for you to remove it completely. When refitting a battery take care to match up the metal contacts on the battery with those in the body of the camera. A lithium-ion (or more simply li-ion) battery is shown on the right.

# Taking a Photograph

Enthusiastic amateurs and professional photographers who want complete control over the camera may prefer to use the manual settings for shutter speed or aperture size, etc., which control the amount of light reaching the camera's image sensor. However, using the "point and click" method with automatic controls should give results which are more than satisfactory for most purposes.

### Point and Click

Unless you're familiar with all the various settings on a camera, set the mode dial in automatic or simple mode. First obtain the required shot using the monitor, together with the zoom facility. The zoom is controlled by a small lever on the top side of the camera on the right. If necessary the camera can be held vertically rather than horizontally. When you are satisfied with the view, depress the shutter button *half way*. The camera *automatically focuses* on the subject and adjusts the *aperture* and *shutter speed* to give the optimum amount of light *exposure*. Keep the shutter button in the half way position until a green light appears; this means the focus and exposure are set. Now fully depress the shutter button to take the photograph. The image is automatically stored on  the camera's memory card as a JPEG file, as discussed earlier. After a second or two the camera is ready to take another photograph, if necessary.

If you find difficulty in holding the camera steady, consider buying a tripod costing £15 upwards. This will eliminate camera shake.

# Reviewing a Photograph

Now set the camera to playback mode by turning the mode dial or by pressing the playback button, usually marked with a triangular "play" icon. Your latest photograph should appear on the monitor, as shown on the next page. You can use the zoom lever to zoom in and the arrow buttons to scroll the image in playback mode. If you're happy with the image, re-set the mode to automatic and you're ready to take some more photographs.

# Deleting an Image from the Memory Card

If you don't wish to keep the image it can easily be deleted with the camera in playback mode. Press the delete button (usually denoted by a picture of a dustbin). Then use the arrow keys to move to **Yes** before pressing the **MENU** or **OK** button to delete the image. Please note there are also options to delete multiple images from the card or to delete all images on the card.

## Making a Movie with a Digital Camera

Compact digital cameras can record moving video and sound, lasting from several minutes to about an hour. On some cameras, video mode is selected using the movie icon on the mode dial. To start filming, press the shutter button as if taking a still photograph. To stop recording, press the shutter button again. Some cameras use a separate video button to start and stop filming.

The video can now be played back on the monitor or on a television set. The video is saved as a file on the memory card alongside those of the still images. After copying to a computer the video can be viewed full screen in the Windows Media Player, with controls for play, stop, pause and sound, etc., as shown along the bottom  of the screenshot below.

## Working With Photographic Images

Once you've taken your photographs and videos, you can review them on the monitor on the back of the camera and delete any you don't want. Otherwise the photographs will remain stored on your camera's memory card until you physically delete them as described earlier.

Once back at home you can:

- View the pictures on a television screen (using a special cable provided with the camera).

- Alternatively, connect your camera or memory card to a special *photo frame* (a sort of electronic picture frame with a remote control) allowing you to view your photos.

- Download the pictures to your computer .

- Save the pictures on your hard disc.

- View them on the computer monitor.

- Enhance and edit the pictures using digital editing software such as the Windows Live Photo Gallery.

- Print the pictures yourself on glossy photographic paper.

- Send them over the Internet to a printing service like Jessops and obtain high quality prints by post.

- E-mail them to a friend or relative.

- Post the pictures onto a photo sharing Web site for others to view, such as Flickr or Facebook, etc.

- Organise and categorize the images into structured folders and albums on the hard disc.

- Archive the pictures securely and permanently by backing them up on a CD or DVD.

The above topics are covered in more detail in the remaining chapters of this book.

# Bits, Bytes and Pixels Explained

Some of the jargon associated with computing and digital photography can be confusing but it's actually quite straightforward, as the notes below attempt to show.

The digital camera and digital computer are so-called because they represent their data (text, pictures, etc.,) electronically using only the digits 0 and 1. These are known as *binary digits* or *bits* for short. Binary means based on the number 2, rather than 10 as in the normal decimal system. Photos stored on the camera's memory card as binary digits are in the correct format to be input into a digital computer and saved on the computer's hard disc.

### Bytes, etc.

Bits are normally handled in groups of 8 known as *bytes*. One byte might represent a letter of the alphabet or the smallest element of a photo, known as a *pixel*, as discussed below.

  1 kilobyte (KB) is 1024 bytes.

  1 megabyte (MB) is approx. 1 million bytes. (1,048,576)

  1 gigabyte (GB) is approx. 1 billion bytes, (1,073,741, 824)

  1 gigabyte is 1024 megabytes.

  A typical photograph may be 3MB in size.

  Memory cards range in capacity from 2 — 32GB.

### Pixels

A *pixel* is a small square *picture element*, one of millions used to make up a photographic image.

  A black or white pixel consists of 8 bits or 1 byte.

  A colour pixel consists of 24 bits or 3 bytes.

  A megapixel (MP) is approximately one million pixels. (1,048,576).

  Modern cameras have a typical resolution of 14MP.

  The resolution can be set at different levels, such as 2MP.

# 3

# Connecting the Memory Card to a Computer

## Introduction

The last chapter described the taking of photos and storing them as image files on the memory card. Although you can have a quick preview of them on the monitor on the back of the camera, you'll probably want to do a lot more with them. Some of the options for using the images on a memory card are as follows:

- Connect the camera to a TV set and view the images, slide shows and videos on the big screen. A special cable for this should be provided with the camera.

- Remove the memory card and insert it in a photo printer to make immediate colour prints.

- Remove the memory card and view the images in an electronic photo frame.

- Take the card to one of the photo processing companies to have the images printed.

- E-mail the photos to an online printing service and have your prints posted back to you.

- Connect your camera or memory card to your computer and save the images on your hard disc, where they can be viewed, edited, printed, sent around the world on the Internet and backup duplicate copies made for security.

This chapter looks at the way a digital camera and more precisely its memory card can be connected to a computer and treated as another disc drive. Then the photographs can be viewed prior to storing copies on the hard disc drive, as described in Chapter 4.

# Making the Connection

### Built-in Card Reader

Many new computers and printers have a built-in card reader. This is a slot or slots in the front of the computer or printer. A brand new computer may be supplied with a dummy memory card in the slot to keep it clean. Simply remove the card from the camera as described in the last chapter and push it gently into the card reader slot in the computer or printer. The computer will automatically detect the card and present a menu of options for importing the images to your computer. This is discussed shortly.

### Downloading Via a USB (Universal Serial Bus) Port

Many computers built a few years ago don't have a built-in memory card reader. However, as long as you have at least one spare USB port on your computer, there are numerous methods and cheap devices for transferring images to your computer. The USB ports are usually on the side of a laptop computer and on the front or back of a desktop computer as shown on the right.

### Adding Extra USB Ports

Apart from connecting cameras the USB ports are used for attaching all sorts of devices to computers these days, such as printers, external disc drives, flash drives, keyboards, and mice, for example. So if you're running short of USB ports, you can buy a cheap adaptor which converts a single USB port into several more, as shown below.

**The USB Cable**

Your camera should be supplied with a cable which connects the camera via a small slot in the camera to a USB port on the computer. This is probably the quickest method but it's not very convenient if you want to look at several memory cards or your camera's battery needs recharging.

As mentioned before, the computer will detect the camera when it's switched on and you will be presented with a menu of downloading options as discussed shortly.

Whenever you connect devices such as cameras, flash drives, etc., the computer will, if necessary, automatically install some special software known as *device drivers*. Then the device, such as a camera, will appear in the Windows Explorer, just like a hard disc drive or CD/DVD drive, etc. This is discussed in more detail shortly.

**External Card Readers**

These are very handy if you don't  have a built-in card reader and prefer to look at the photographs with the memory card out of the camera. This would be the case if you have several different memory cards and you wanted to browse through them. Shown above on the right is a card reader in the form of a "dongle" which plugs directly into a USB port. An 8GB memory card is shown inserted into the card reader above. This particular card reader is designed to accommodate the popular SD memory card but there are card readers to suit various other shapes and sizes of memory card.

The Kingston card reader shown  on the right connects to the computer using a USB cable. There are various slots to accommodate different memory cards such as SD, CompactFlash and Memory Stick.

After you insert the card reader into a vacant USB port on the first occasion, the computer detects it and installs the necessary software. The computer searches an Internet resource known as Windows Update for the correct "device driver" software, to enable the card reader to work with your computer. In exceptional cases when installing a new device, if a suitable driver can't be found by Windows, or you don't have the manufacturer's software CD, log on to the Web site of the manufacturer of the device. Then download the correct driver for your particular version of Windows, such as XP, Vista or Windows 7. It's usually a case of selecting the **Support** section of their Web site and then selecting **Download drivers**.

# Examining the Memory Card

One of the advantages of connecting devices via a USB port is that they can be "hot swapped", i.e. plugged in while the computer is up and running. As soon as you connect the camera or memory card reader, the device is quickly detected and the memory card effectively becomes like another disc drive in the computer. As shown on page 30, the **Autoplay** menu appears, displaying a list of options for importing your photos to the computer or viewing them on the screen. These are discussed in detail shortly.

To see how the memory card appears on the computer, click the Windows Explorer icon on the Taskbar at the bottom left of the screen and shown  here on the right. Now select **Computer** from the left-hand side of the Explorer window to display the various disc drives connected to this computer.

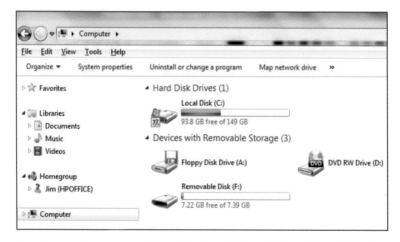

As shown above, apart from the hard drive **(C:)** and the **DVD RW Drive (D:)**, etc., the memory card has been assigned the name **Removable Disk (F:)**. In this case it is a **7.39GB** card (nominally 8GB) most of which is still free.

# The AutoPlay Menu

After you've connected the complete camera or just the memory card to the computer by one of the methods described earlier, the computer detects the memory card and should very quickly display the **AutoPlay** menu shown below.

### Opening the AutoPlay Menu

If the **AutoPlay** menu doesn't appear as shown above, click the Windows Explorer icon shown on the right, found on the Taskbar at the bottom left of the screen. Then right-click the name or icon for the memory card in the Windows Explorer. It will probably be labelled  **Removable Disk (E:)** or **(F:)**. From the menu which appears click **Open AutoPlay...** as shown on the right to display the **Autoplay** menu.

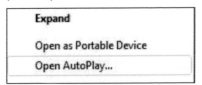

# Viewing Photos in the Windows Explorer

As can be seen from the top of the **AutoPlay** menu, the camera's memory card is designated **Removable Disk (F:)**. The **Autoplay** menu has various options to view or import photos to a computer.

Click **Open folder to view files using Windows Explorer** on the **Autoplay** menu shown on the previous page to see how your camera has saved your photos as files in folders on the memory card, displayed in the Windows Explorer, as shown below.

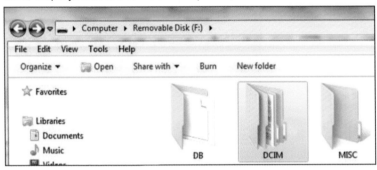

The folder **DCIM** contains the photos and double clicking this shows that there are two sub-folders **103_PANA** and **104OLYMP** as shown below. (This card has been used in a Panasonic and an Olympus camera, each creating their own folder).

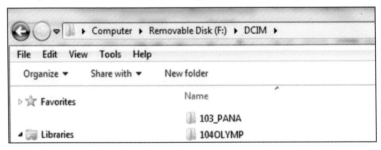

If you now double-click the **PANA** folder, the images on the memory card taken with the Panasonic camera are displayed, as shown on the next page.

At this stage the images are still on the memory card and have not yet been copied to the computer's hard disc drive. The file names such as **P1030063.JPG** were assigned by the camera; these can be changed to more meaningful names as discussed later. The letters **.JPG** represent the standard format used for saving photographs as files on memory cards and disc drives. These are also known as JPEG files, a format agreed by a technical body known as the Joint Photographic Experts Group.

If you are already familiar with managing computer files, you could right-click over one of the images and use the menu which appears to carry out a variety of operations on the image such as copying, deleting and renaming. These file management tasks are discussed in Chapter 10 of this book.

**The Memory Card as a General Storage Device**

Although this book has only shown the memory card as a medium for saving photographs in a digital camera, it is in fact a versatile storage device. The memory card, when connected to a computer, can be used like a disc drive, flash drive or CD-RW for saving and deleting  files such as text or music, for example.

# Viewing Photos in the Photo Gallery

The **Autoplay** menu shown below and on page 30 has another option allowing you to view the images saved on the memory card. Click **View pictures using Windows Live Photo Gallery** as shown below.

The Windows Live Photo Gallery opens displaying the first image on the card, as shown on the next page.

The above **View pictures** option is only available if you have downloaded the free Windows Live Photo Gallery as described on page 10 of this book. In the above **AutoPlay** menu, there is also an option **Organize and Edit using Adobe Photoshop Elements**. This won't appear unless you have installed the Adobe Photoshop Elements program on your computer.

As shown above the pictures are displayed one at a time in the Photo Gallery window. The icons at the bottom right above and shown enlarged below represent various ways of viewing the images.

Reading from left to right, the first two icons allow you to display the previous image and next image. The next two icons enable the image to be rotated left and right. Clicking the red cross deletes the current image. The icon in the middle representing a screen launches a slide show which automatically displays all of the images in sequence one at a time.

The icon on the right causes the photograph to be switched between two sizes, actual size and the image resized to fit the Photo Gallery window.

Finally the slider on the right above can be dragged using the mouse to zoom in and zoom out of the image,

# Connecting a Camera Phone

Many mobile phones include a digital camera capable of taking good quality photographs. The phone itself may have the ability to save and delete photos and e-mail them to friends or post them to social networking Web sites such as Facebook or Twitter. However, you might prefer to transfer copies of photos to your computer, for editing, printing or archiving to a CD-R, etc.

Your digital phone package might include a cable to connect your phone to a computer via a USB port as discussed earlier.

When you connect the phone to the computer using a USB cable and switch on, the phone is detected. If the **AutoPlay** menu appears, click one of the **View** options as described earlier. Alternatively launch the Windows Explorer, as shown below, by clicking its icon shown on the right on the Windows Taskbar at the bottom of the screen.

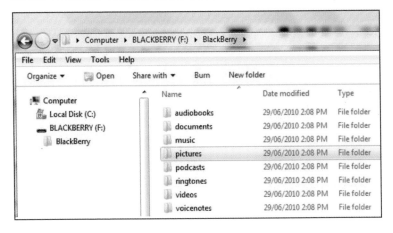

When you double-click the **BlackBerry\pictures** folder shown on the previous page, the Windows Explorer shows the images which have been saved on the phone, as shown below.

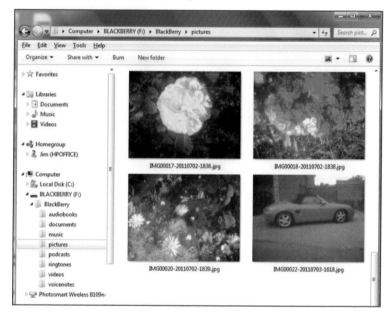

In the above example, the images are displayed as **Extra large icons**. This can be selected in the Windows Explorer from the **View** menu on the menu bar as shown below.

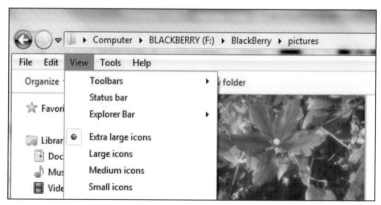

# Copying Photographs and Videos to a Computer

## Introduction

The previous chapter showed various methods of connecting a camera's memory card to a computer; also how to view the photos on the computer screen while they are still on the card. This allows you to decide which images you want to import to the computer and to save permanently on the hard disc drive.

It should be pointed out that even when the images are saved on your hard disc drive, they are not completely safe. For example, folders on the hard disc drive can be accidentally deleted; additionally a technical problem may require the hard disc drive to be *formatted or* "wiped" and the software reinstalled. This could mean the loss of your photographs — quite a disaster if they record important events such as a wedding or social occasion. Methods of making secure, duplicate backup copies of important photographs are discussed later in this book.

The Windows operating system makes it easy to copy your images to a computer and save them on the hard disc drive. The **AutoPlay** menu described in the previous chapter has two options for importing photographs and saving and organising them in labelled folders and these are described shortly.

Alternatively it's not difficult to create your own system of named folders and then store photographs in them using "copy" and "paste" in the Windows Explorer. This results in a more personal system, making it easier to find and manage your photos. These topics are covered in the remainder of this book.

Video clips are saved in a different file format but are copied to the computer in exactly the same way as still photographs.

# Using Windows to Import Photographs

Connect the memory card to your computer, either in the camera or using a memory card reader as discussed in the last chapter. The **AutoPlay** menu should appear as shown below. If the menu doesn't open automatically, it can be launched from the Windows Explorer as described at the bottom of page 30.

Click **Import pictures and videos using Windows** shown above and the following window appears. You can insert an optional tag such as **Rome** in this example. This will precede the names of the photographs when they are saved as files on the hard disc drive. Then click the **Import** button shown below.

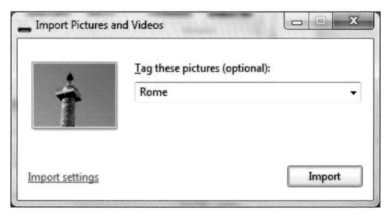

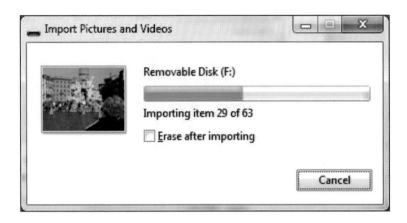

You are informed of progress as the copying of the photographs proceeds. Clicking the **Erase after importing** check box, shown above, causes the images to be deleted from the camera's memory card. At the end of the copying process, the copies of the images are stored by default in the folder **C:\Users\Jim\My Pictures** on the hard disc drive as shown below.

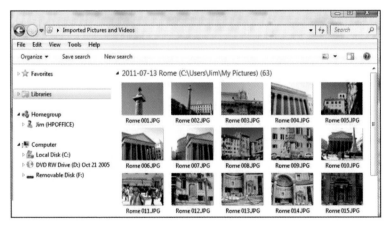

Each image was numbered previously by the camera as in **014** above and saved on the memory card as a **.jpg** file. The name **Rome** was added as a Tag as shown on the previous page.

# Checking the Saved Photographs

The photographs have now been copied to the hard disc drive (**C:**). In order to work with them at a later date, such as viewing, editing, printing or sharing with other people, you need to be able to find them quickly and easily. Click the Windows Explorer icon on the Taskbar at the bottom of the screen, as shown on the right. Then click **Libraries** and double-click the **Pictures Library** icon.

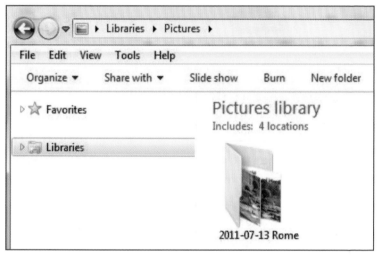

To examine the photographs just copied to the hard disc drive, double-click the folder **2011-07-13 Rome**. This displays all the photographs as icons in the Windows Explorer as shown with the file named **Rome 043.JPG** on the right. Click **View** on the menu bar shown above to display the images as icons in different sizes or to display details such as file size, file type and date taken.

Now the images are all copied to the hard disc there are many ways they can be viewed, edited, printed, organised and shared as discussed later in this book.

# Using the Photo Gallery to Import Photos

The **AutoPlay** menu has an option, shown below, which allows you to import the images using the Windows Live Photo Gallery. (Details for downloading the free Photo Gallery software from the Internet are given on page 10.)

When you click **Import pictures and videos using Windows Live Photo Gallery** shown above, the Photo Gallery discovers all the "new" photos on the memory card. (Images on the card which have been imported before are not counted). The **Review** option below allows you to arrange the images in groups, add a title to each group and select which images are to be imported.

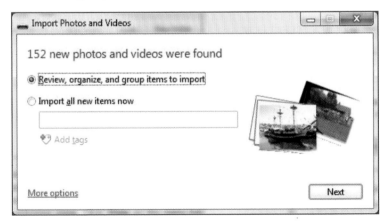

After clicking **Next**, the following window appears.

The photos can be arranged in groups according to the date and time they were taken. The slider shown at the bottom right above allows you to change the amount of time between groups and therefore the number of groups. With the slider in the extreme right position, all of the photos are in one group as shown above. There is a check box which allows you to select all of the photos and import them or you can click and tick individual photos to be imported. You can also click **Enter a name** and supply a name for the folder in which the group of images will be stored.

If you click **More options** shown above you can **Browse** for a folder on the hard disc drive into which the images will be copied. Otherwise the folder **My Pictures** will be used by default, as shown on the next page. The files can be saved with the original file name assigned by the camera and you can also add the date.

As shown above you can choose an option for the Windows Live Photo Gallery to open as soon as the photos have been imported to the hard disc drive. There is also a box to delete the imported photos from the original source i.e. the camera's memory card.

After you click the **Import** button, the **Import Photos and Videos** window appears as shown below, informing you of progress.

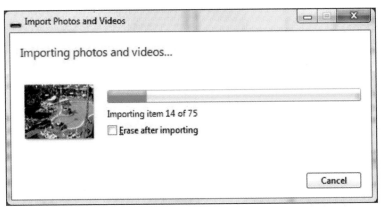

After the images have all been imported, by default the Windows Live Photo Gallery opens displaying the photographs, as shown below. The photographs are now permanently saved on the hard disc and can now be deleted from the camera's memory card, (unless you already chose this option during the import process).

In this example, the folder was given the name **Tenerife** and in total 75 photos were copied. (Some images were subsequently deleted, leaving only 59 in this particular group.) As shown above, the sub-folder **Tenerife** appears in the **My Pictures** folder within the **Pictures Library**. You can view these photographs in the Windows Live Photo Gallery at a later date by clicking the **Start** button at the bottom left of the screen and shown on the right, then click the **All Programs** menu and select **Windows Live Photo Gallery**.

Alternatively click the Windows Explorer icon shown on the right, select **Libraries** and double-click the **Pictures Library** folder.

# The Import Option on the Photo Gallery Ribbon

Launch the program by clicking the **Start** button shown on the right and then selecting **All Programs** and **Windows Live Photo Gallery**.

Now connect your camera to the computer using a USB cable and switch the camera on. Alternatively remove the memory card from the camera and connect it to the computer using a card reader as discussed in the previous chapter.

From the left of the Photo Gallery menu bar click **Import** as shown on the right and on the previous page. The **Import Photos and Videos** window opens as shown below. The blue icon represents an Olympus camera, **Removable Disk (E:)** is a memory card inserted in a printer and **HP Photosmart** is a printer containing a scanner.

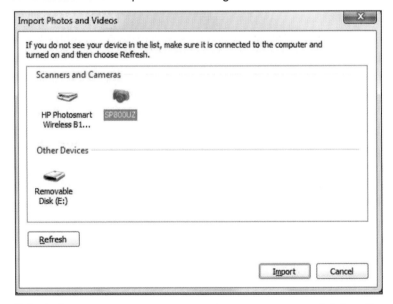

Select the camera, memory card or scanner containing the images and click the **Import** button.

When you click the **Import** button shown on the previous page, the Photo Gallery searches for photographs on the memory card. You are then presented with the **Import Photos and Videos** window as shown below.

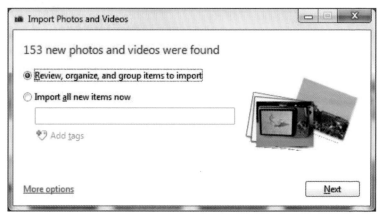

This allows you to organize the photos into groups and add a name for the destination folder on the computer's hard disc drive.

When you click **Next** the images are imported and finally displayed in the Windows Live Photo Gallery as described earlier in this chapter.

# Scanning Old Photographic Prints

You may have some old photographic prints, which you want to send by e-mail to friends and relatives around the world. Or you might want to edit them and incorporate them in a document produced on your computer. Using an inexpensive scanner, they can be "digitised", i.e. converted to digital images in the JPEG (.jpg) file format discussed earlier. Then they are ready to be imported to a computer and suitable for sending around the Internet. Many inexpensive multi-function printers now have a built-in scanner or you can buy a standalone "flatbed" scanner.

In this example, the scanner is part of an HP Photosmart Inkjet Wireless printer. Place the photograph face down on the bed on the top of the scanner. Launch the Windows Live Photo Gallery program as previously described and click the **Import** icon shown on the right and on the Photo Gallery menu bar shown at the bottom of the previous page. The **Import Photos and Videos** window opens showing a blue icon  representing the **Wireless** printer and scanner.

When you click the **Import** button shown at the bottom of the previous page, the **New Scan** window opens as shown below. Click the **Preview** button to have a preliminary look at the scanned image as shown below.

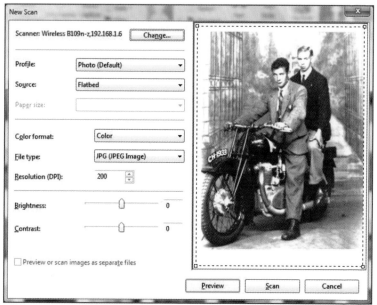

Now click the **Scan** button  and the **Import Pictures and Videos** window opens as shown on the next page. You can add a tag to the picture and also click **Import settings** to make various changes to the import process. These include changing the main destination folder where the image will be saved on the hard disc drive. By default this is **My Pictures** as shown at the bottom of the next page.

**Creating Your own Folders**

As discussed in Chapter 10, you can easily create your own hierarchy of folders for storing images on the hard disc drive. These can have names which are meaningful to you and help you to keep track of your images.

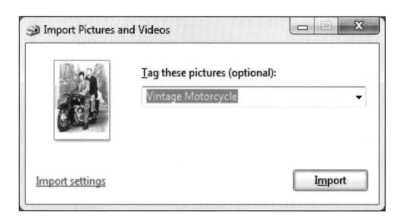

After clicking **Import**, the Windows Explorer opens automatically, displaying an icon for the scanned image and the tag as part of the file name. The file location is **C:\Users\Jim\My Pictures**.

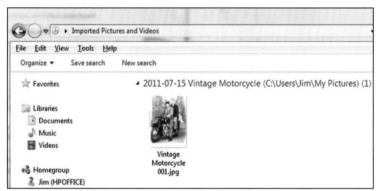

 To access this image at a later time, click the Windows Explorer icon on the left of the Taskbar at the bottom of the screen. Then click **Libraries** and double-click **Pictures Library**. The scanned image appears in its own folder, as shown on the right. Double-click this folder to return to the view of the file in the Windows Explorer shown above.

# The Stored Photographic Image File

This chapter has shown how photographic images can be copied from the camera's memory card and saved as files on the hard disc drive, such as the scanned photograph saved with the file name **Vintage Motorcycle 001.jpg**. The location of this photograph on the hard disc drive is:

Vintage
Motorcycle
001.jpg

C:\Users\Jim\My Pictures

**C:\** is the abbreviation for the hard disc drive. **Users** and **My Pictures** are folders within the Windows operating system. **Jim** is a folder created automatically by Windows when I first became a user of the computer. The full pathname to this photograph is:

C:\Users\Jim\My Pictures\Vintage Motorcycle 001.jpg

**Working With Photos Stored on the Hard Disc Drive**

Many tasks are now possible, using software such as the free Windows Live Photo Gallery and the Windows Explorer:

- Edit and improve images, "crop" to delete unwanted material and remove effects such as "red eye".
- View photographs on the computer screen individually or as an automatic slide show.
- Make your own prints on glossy paper.
- Order high quality prints using an online printing service.
- Share photos with friends and family around the world by sending with e-mails or by posting to an Internet Web site such as Flickr or Facebook.
- Incorporate photos into documents such as magazines.
- Manage and organize your photos into your own categories making them easy to locate in the future.
- Create secure archives which cannot easily be lost.

The above topics are discussed in the remainder of this book.

# Viewing Photographs and Videos on a Computer

## Locating Photos on the Hard Disc Drive

Previous chapters showed how to copy the images from your camera to the hard disc drive of a computer. You'll probably want to have a good look at the new photos; then you might want to delete a few, improve some by editing and then print them. You might also want to share them with other people using e-mail and the Internet as discussed later.

As described in the previous chapter, the photographs are stored by default in a folder on the hard disc drive called **My Pictures** within the **Pictures Library**. This can be opened by clicking the Windows Explorer icon shown on the right, on the Taskbar at the bottom left of the screen. Then click **Libraries** and double-click the **Pictures Library** folder.

Alternatively the photographs can be accessed by a different route in the Windows Explorer using the following hierarchy of folders:

### C:\Users\Jim\My Pictures

To find this location click the **Start** button, then click **Computer** (Windows XP users click **My Computer**) then double-click the hard disc drive (**C:**). Alternatively click the Windows Explorer icon shown above and double-click the hard disc drive (**C:**).

Next scroll down and double-click the **Users** folder, followed by the sub-folder having your user name, instead of **Jim** in this example. Finally double-click the folder **My Pictures** to display the folders of photographs as shown on the next page.

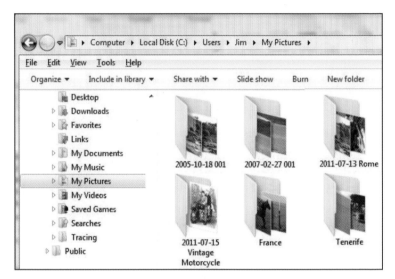

## The Folders Containing the Photos

As shown above, the folders are labelled in slightly different ways, depending on the method used to import them, as discussed in the previous chapter. It's a simple matter to rename a folder after right-clicking its name or icon as shown above. File and folder management tasks such as this are discussed in more detail in Chapter 10. Double-click a folder such as **2011-07-13 Rome** above, to display the names and icons for the images.

## Displaying the Images as Icons

The photographs are displayed as **Large icons**, as shown at the top of the next page. The **View** menu on the Windows Explorer menu bar shown on the right allows you to display the icons and file names of the photographs in various ways. An extract from the **View** menu is shown on the right. Click **View** and then select the type of display you want.

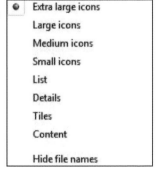

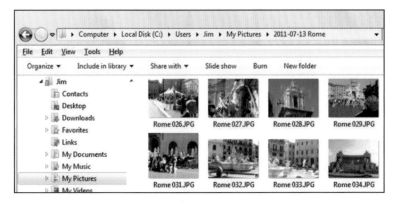

The **Extra large icons** display shown below gives you a very good preview of the images before viewing them full screen.

### Displaying the Images as a List With Details

The **Details** option on the **View** menu shown at the bottom of the previous page gives information such as the date the photo was taken, the file type and the size of the file.

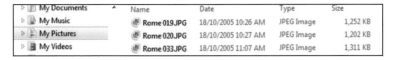

Click the header on the top of a column such as **Name**, **Date** or **Size** to arrange the list of images in order, such as alphabetical, date taken or ascending or descending order of size.

# Viewing Photographs on the Screen

Locate the folder containing the required photograph as just described, either in the default folder **My Pictures** or in a folder you have created on the hard disc drive, as discussed later. Click the required image and the Windows Explorer menu bar displays the **Preview** menu shown below. (Some configurations use **Open** instead of **Preview**). If you click the small downward pointing arrow to the right of **Preview** or **Open**, a list of programs is displayed. These are all programs which can be used to display photographs and the list will vary on different computers.

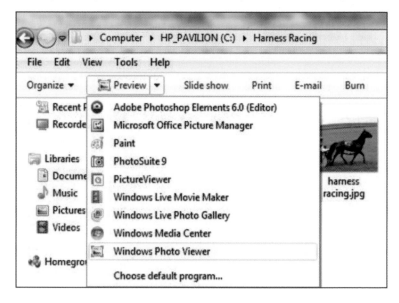

The **Windows Photo Viewer**, the **Windows Live Photo Gallery** and the **Paint** program shown above are three very useful Microsoft programs for viewing photographs and are discussed in detail in this book. Several of the other programs such as the **PhotoSuite** and **Adobe Photoshop Elements** will not appear on your computer unless you've installed them yourself.

**The Default Photo Viewing Program**

On your computer this will probably be the Windows Photo Viewer or the Windows Live Photo Gallery. Click the arrow to the right of **Preview** shown on the previous page. Then select **Choose default program....**

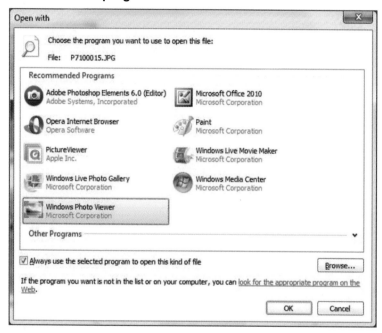

Select the program you want to use to open photographs by default, such as the **Windows Photo Viewer**, if it's not already set as the default. Click **OK** to set the default program.

Now you can open a picture in the default viewing program by clicking **Preview** or **Open** from the Windows Explorer menu bar shown on the previous page.

> **Please note that a quick way to open a photograph for viewing in the default program is to double-click its icon in the Windows Explorer.**

### Opening a Photograph in the  Default Program

Open the folder containing the photograph after clicking
the Windows Explorer icon shown on the right and on
the Taskbar at the bottom left of the screen. Now select
the icon for the photograph so that it's highlighted
against a coloured background. Next click **Preview**
or **Open** from the Windows Explorer menu bar.

Alternatively double-click the icon for the program
in the Windows Explorer.

The photograph opens in the default viewing program, in this
case the Windows Photo Viewer, as shown above.

The Windows Photo Viewer has a menu bar across the top as shown below.

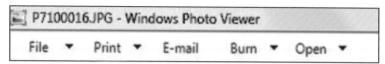

These menus are discussed later in the section on the Windows Live Photo Gallery, which has a very similar menu bar.

The Taskbar along the bottom of the Windows Photo Viewer has a set of controls for the viewing of photographs.

Clicking the magnifying glass icon on the left above displays a slider which can be dragged to change the size of the display. The next icon, shown on the right "toggles", i.e. switches, between the actual image size (very large) and a size which just fits inside the Photo Viewer window as shown on the previous page.

The two arrow buttons shown on the right allow you to display the previous and next photographs in the folder.

The icon on the centre displays all of the photographs (in the current folder) one at a time in an automatically changing slide show. This is discussed in more detail on the next page.

The two circular arrows rotate the image through 90 degrees counter clockwise and clockwise respectively, reading from left to right.

Finally the red cross icon can be used to delete the image from the hard disc.

# Viewing Photographs in a Slide Show

The slide show changes the photographs automatically, such as while you are describing them to friends or relatives. Or you might want to give a talk to a local history society or gardening club, for example. It's easy to connect a projector to a laptop computer so that the pictures can be viewed on a larger screen.

A slide show can be launched from the Windows Picture Viewer as previously described. You can also launch a slide show from the Windows Explorer.  Open the Windows Explorer by clicking its icon on the left of the Taskbar at the bottom of the screen. Then open the folder containing the photos to be included in the slide show.

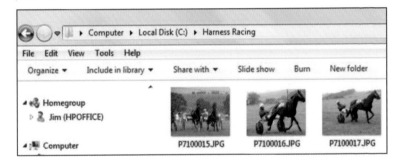

Click **Slide show** on the Windows Explorer menu bar shown above. The first picture is displayed on its own, filling the whole screen without any program windows, menu bars or icons, etc.

After a short time the next photo takes over the whole screen and this process is repeated until all of the photographs in the folder have been displayed.

There are various settings to control the slide show. These settings can be changed using a menu which pops up when you right-click anywhere over one of the photographs during a slide show, as shown on the next page.

The pop-up settings menu for the slide show is shown above after right-clicking the screen during a slide show. For clarity, the menu is shown again enlarged, on the right. During a talk, you might want to use **Pause** to talk at length about a particular photo and you can move back or forwards using **Back** and **Next**.

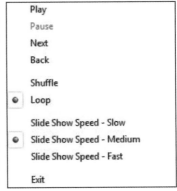

**Shuffle** changes the order in which the images are displayed. With **Loop** switched on as shown above, the slide show is repeated after all of the photographs in a folder have been displayed.

There are 3 speed settings **Slow**, **Medium** and **Fast** to control how long an image is displayed for. Click **Exit** to close the menu.

To end a slide show and return to the Windows Explorer, press the **Escape** (**Esc**) key.

# Using Your Photographs as a Screen Saver

A screen saver is a constantly changing pattern or set of images displayed automatically if your computer is not used for a while. The screen saver was originally intended to protect early monitors from damage if the same image was displayed on the screen for a long time; nowadays screen savers are used more for amusement or privacy. So for example, while your computer is not being used for a time, it can provide an automatic backdrop of all your favourite family, holiday, sporting or wildlife photographs, for example.

Click the **Start** button shown on the right and then select **Control Panel** and **Appearance and Personalization**. Next under **Personalization** click **Change screen saver**.

The **Screen Saver Settings** window appears as shown below. From the drop-down menu under **Screen saver**, select **Windows Live Photo Gallery** as shown below.

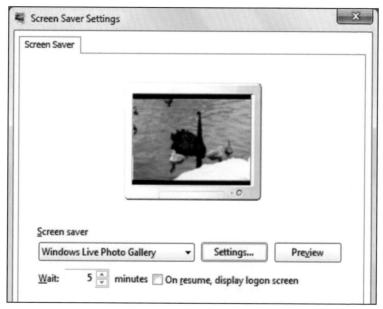

By default the screen saver will use all of the photos in your Windows Live Photo Gallery. The **Preview** button shown on the previous page gives a full-screen demonstration of the photos. As shown at the bottom of the window on the previous page, you can set the period of computer inactivity before the screen saver is displayed. This is set at 5 minutes by default. The **Settings...** button allows you to fine tune the screen saver as shown below.

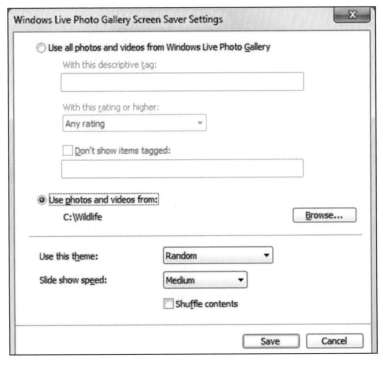

As shown above, you can use all of the photos in your Windows Live Photo Gallery or you can use **Browse...** and then just use a selected folder such as **C:\Wildlife** in this example. You can also change the **Slide show speed**. **Shuffle** changes the order the images are displayed in.

The drop-down menu to the right of **Use this theme:** on the **Screen Saver Settings** menu on the previous page provides graphical effects such as Collage and Album shown below.

**Screen Saver Using the Collage Theme**

**Screen Saver Using the Album Theme**

# Viewing Video Clips on Your Computer

As mentioned previously, you can record video clips using a digital camera by selecting the film strip icon on the camera's mode dial and pressing the shutter button to start and stop the recording. Alternatively some cameras have a separate button to start and stop the recording. The video is saved on the camera's memory card automatically but in a different file format from the still photographs discussed earlier. Common video file formats used with digital cameras are the **.MOV (**Apple QuickTime), **.AVI** (Audio Video Interleave) and **.WMV** (Windows Media Video).

Open the Windows Explorer by clicking the icon on the Taskbar, shown on the right. Then double-click the folder containing the required video clip, as shown below for the **Otter.MOV** video in the folder **C:\Wildlife**.

As shown below, the video **Otter.MOV** file is saved in the Windows Explorer alongside the icons for **.JPG** still photographs.

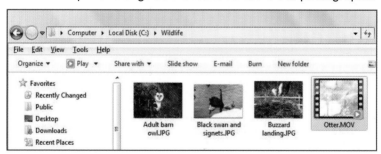

When you select the **Otter.MOV** video icon, the **Preview** option on the toolbar across the top of the Explorer window changes to **Play**, as shown above. Clicking the small downward pointing arrow to the right of **Play** above presents a list of media playing programs which should be able to play this video.

**iTunes**, **QuickTime Player** and **RealPlayer** are all media player programs which can be downloaded free to your computer from the Internet. **Windows Media Player** is part of Microsoft Windows and **Windows Live Movie Maker** can be downloaded free, as described for **Windows Live Photo Gallery** on page 10.

The Windows Live Movie Maker contains many tools for editing videos and adding special effects. The Windows Media Player can play common video types such as **.MOV** and **.AVI** and you could, if necessary, set this as your default video player as discussed on page 55 for viewing still photographs. When you click **Play** on the Explorer Toolbar or double-click the video icon such as **Otter.MOV** in Windows Explorer, the Windows Media Player opens ready to play the video clip, as shown below.

As shown above there are control buttons to play, pause, stop, forward, rewind, volume/mute and display the video full screen. This video clip lasted 35 seconds and had a file size of 48MB.

# A Tour of Windows Live Photo Gallery 2011

## Introduction

Windows Live Photo Gallery contains everything you need to manage, edit and share your digital photographs using a computer and is available as a free download from the Internet. Among its many facilities are:

- Importing photos from a camera or card reader, etc.
- Displaying images, including viewing as a slide show.
- Editing photographs to improve quality or remove defects, blemishes and unwanted material (cropping).
- Organizing images in folders with captions and tags to make finding particular pictures very fast and easy.
- Combining several photos into a single panoramic view.
- Sharing images by printing, e-mailing, posting to Web sites such as SkyDrive, Facebook and Flickr.
- Copying images to a CD or DVD as a safe archive.

Windows Live Photo Gallery is part of a suite of programs known as Windows Live Essentials. As described on page 10 of this book, these can be downloaded from the **Essentials** section of the following Web site:

### http://**explore**.live.com

There is one version of the Windows Live Photo Gallery 2011 for Windows 7 and Vista and another for Windows XP.

# Launching the Windows Live Photo Gallery

The program is launched by clicking the **Start** button at the bottom left of the screen and shown on the right. Then click **All Programs** followed by **Windows Live**

**Photo Gallery**. Alternatively the **Windows Live Photo Gallery** may already be listed in the **Start** menu itself. To include **Windows Live Photo**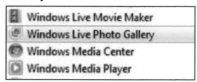

Gallery in the **Start** menu, right-click over its entry in the **All Programs** menu and select **Pin to Start Menu**, as shown below.

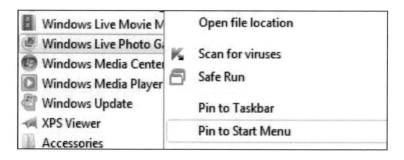

A good way to launch a program quickly using only a single click is to place an icon for the program on the Taskbar at the bottom of the screen, as shown below.

To place the icon (shown right) for the **Windows Live Photo Gallery** on the Taskbar, right-click over **Windows Live Photo Gallery** in the **All Programs** menu and select **Pin to Taskbar** as shown above.

To remove the icon from the Taskbar at a later date, right-click over the icon and select **Unpin this program from taskbar**.

# The Photo Gallery Screen

After launching the program as described on the previous page, the Windows Live Photo Gallery opens displaying icons for your photos in the **My Pictures** folder, as described in Chapter 4.

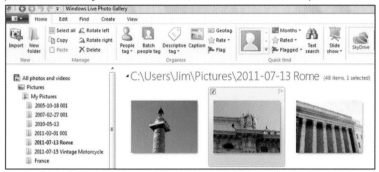

Across the top of the screen is the Ribbon, a recent Microsoft innovation which displays the various tools as icons on several tabs such as **Home**, **Edit**, **Find**, etc. This largely replaces the traditional menu bar which uses **File**, **Edit** and **View**, etc.

On the left-hand panel above are the various folders which the Photo Gallery has created for storing photos during importing as discussed in Chapter 4. Click any of the folders to display the photos as icons or *thumbnails* in the main panel in the centre.

A number of icons appear on the Taskbar at the bottom right of the screen, as shown below. These perform various operations on a photo which has been selected by clicking. A selected photo is highlighted in blue as shown in the Photo Gallery above.

The two icons shown on the left above rotate the photo through 90 degrees, left and right respectively. Clicking the red cross icon shown above deletes the image from the Photo Gallery.

## The Photo Gallery Slide Show

The icon on the right starts a slide show of all the images in the current folder, as shown below.

There are controls to pause and stop the slide show and you can choose from a number of themes, as shown on the right. The menu headings appear when you pass the cursor over the top of the slide show screen. The themes alter the way the images are displayed and how they are changed, e.g. by panning and zooming or fading into the next image. There are also options to create a movie with the photos and videos and to share them on the Web. (Sharing photos and videos is discussed later). A slide show can be closed by pressing the Escape key or by clicking **Back to Photo Gallery** in the top right-hand corner of the screen, just visible above.

## Changing the Icon Size

You can change the size of the icons or thumbnails in the Photo Gallery by dragging the slider shown below on the right.

## Displaying Details of Photographs

The small icon on the left of the slider, shown above and on the right, switches on a display of details of each of the photos, as shown below. The details can be changed during the editing process, discussed shortly.

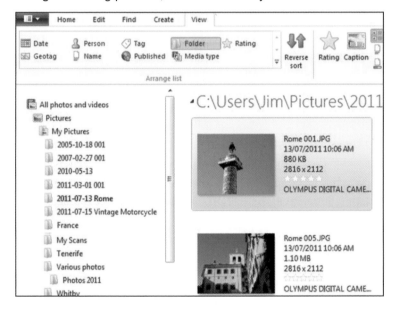

The blue background indicates that the photo has been selected by clicking. The Photo Gallery also displays the exact location of the current sub-folder, e.g., **2011-07-13 Rome** within all of the folders on the hard disc drive or (**C:**) drive, as shown below.

◂C:\Users\Jim\Pictures\2011-07-13 Rome

# The Photo Gallery Ribbon

The Ribbon across the top of the screen contains icons for many of the tasks needed to edit, view, organize, share and print your photographs, as shown below.

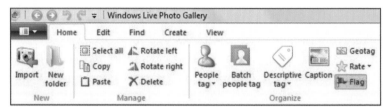

### The Home Tab

The icons on the Ribbon are organized in a series of tabs, namely **Home**, **Edit**, **Find**, **Create** and **View** shown above. When the Photo Gallery first starts up it displays the **Home** tab. As can be seen above, the **Home** tab contains icons for many basic tasks with your photos. Tags and captions are a means of adding extra information to photos, making them easier to organize and find. The icons are arranged in groups such as **New**, **Manage** and **Organize** shown above along the bottom of the ribbon.

The right-hand side of the **Home** tab shown below has a group of icons in the group **Quick find**, used to search for photos meeting certain criteria. Next there is an icon to start a **Slide show**.

The **Share** group of icons on the right above allow you to post your photos on various Web sites such as SkyDrive, Facebook, YouTube and Flickr where they can be viewed by other people. There is also an icon to send photos with an e-mail message. These topics are discussed in more detail later in this book.

## The File Menu

The Ribbon has replaced the traditional menu bar consisting of **File**, **Edit** and **View**, etc., but the Photo Gallery still has a **File** menu on the left-hand side of the Ribbon. This is opened (and closed) by clicking the icon on the left of the **Home** tab and shown here on the right.

As can be seen, the **File** menu contains tools for importing photographs into the Photo Gallery and other important tasks. The **Print** option allows you to make "hard copy" of your photos on paper, with a further option to order prints from an online photo printing service. **Burn** shown on the right copies photos to a CD or DVD. As discussed later, this is a secure way of archiving important photographs which might otherwise be lost or accidentally deleted.

Clicking **Properties** shown on the right above opens a window shown below displaying a huge amount of information about an image selected in the Photo Gallery. (A photo is selected by a single click and appears against a blue background, as shown on page 69). These details include the file name and file type, the file size, the associated program and the location of the folder.

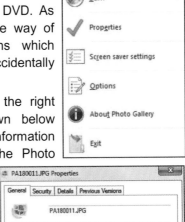

The **File** menu also has a **Screen saver settings** option (described on page 60) and an **Options** feature to change many of the settings controlling the way the Photo Gallery operates.

## The Edit Tab

Clicking the **Edit** tab presents a different set of icons or tools designed for editing photographs as shown below.

Editing is discussed in more detail in Chapter 7, but you can see above that there are tools to make some major changes to images. For example, if you've taken a photo with the camera turned vertically, you'll might want to use one of the **Rotate** options. Similarly, if an image is tilted slightly, you might want to use the **Straighten** tool. Several icons represent tools to improve the colour and quality of a photograph and these can all be applied automatically using the **Auto adjust** icon shown above.

## The Find Tab

Within a short time you might have several thousand photos stored on your hard disc. The **Find** tab shown below allows you to very quickly select and display images meeting certain criteria.

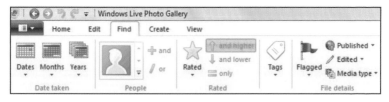

For example, you can pick out images taken on a certain date. The face recognition tag picks out photos containing certain people. Images can be tagged with a name or label when they are being imported or during editing. Clicking the tag in a drop-down list displays only the tagged photos. Similarly you can apply a *flag* to certain photos and later just display the flagged images.

## The Create Tab

The icons on this tab are mainly for using and sharing your photos after they've been edited. Click an image in the Photo Gallery then click **Set as desktop** on the left above. The image provides a background to your Desktop, the screen and all of its icons which appear when the computer first starts up, as shown above.

The **Panorama** tool above "stitches" together two or more images of the same scene to make one wider picture. **Photo Fuse** allows you to merge two similar group photos together so that the best images of a person are used.

**Order prints** displays a list of online photo printing companies. Select the pictures you want printed and click **Send Pictures**. Within a few days the glossy prints will be posted back to you.

**Photo email** presents a choice between sending a photograph embedded within the text of an e-mail or as an *attachment* to an e-mail text message, using your default e-mail program such as the free Windows Live Mail program.

The **Movie** icon above allows you to add photos to a project you are creating with Windows Live Movie Maker.

Most of the other icons are concerned with posting your photos to Web sites such as SkyDrive, Facebook and Flickr. These topics are discussed in detail in Chapter 9.

## The View Tab

The left-hand side of the **View** tab on the Ribbon is shown below.

The icons above in the **Arrange list** section are used to group, sort and list the photos as they are displayed as icons in the Windows Live Photo Gallery. For example, if you select **Rating**, pictures assigned a 5 star rating will appear at the top, followed by 4 star rated pictures, etc. (**Reverse sort** shown above would put the lowest rated pictures at the top of the list). The pictures in the Photo Gallery can also be listed according to the **Date**, **Tag**, **Name** (i.e. file name), **Folder** and where they have been **Published** (Facebook, etc.). Selecting **Media type** above separates the list of icons into **Photos** and **Videos**.

The right-hand side of the **View** tab on the **Ribbon** allows you to control what information, such as **All details**, is displayed against each icon or thumbnail, as shown on the right. There are  also icons to show or hide any **Flags**, to **Zoom in** or **Zoom out**, start a **Slide show** or display the **Tag and caption pane** down the right-hand side of the screen.

# Basic Editing of Digital Photographs

## Introduction

One of the main advantages of digital photography using a computer is that you can improve, modify and polish your pictures without specialised knowledge or equipment. Modern photo editing programs are easy to use and allow complex operations to be carried out with just a few clicks of a mouse. The Windows Live Photo Gallery includes powerful editing tools and, as described on page 10 of this book, is available as a free download from the Internet. Although the Photo Gallery is completely free of charge its facilities are comparable with similar programs costing around £50-£60. Some typical photo editing tasks covered in the next two chapters are as follows:

- Cropping an image to remove unwanted material.

- Rotating and straightening an image.

- Improving the quality of a photo by changing the colours, exposure, contrast, etc.

- Removing blemishes and defects such as "red eye".

- Resizing and resaving in a smaller file size to facilitate posting to a Web site or sending in an e-mail.

- "Stitching" together two or more pictures to make one wide panoramic view of a particular scene.

Changes applied to an image during editing are saved automatically but there is a **Revert to original** button to undo any changes you don't like.

The Photo Gallery is opened by clicking **Start**, **All Programs** and **Windows Live Photo Gallery** (Unless you've placed it on the **Start** menu or pinned it to the Taskbar at the bottom of the screen, as shown on page 66.) Then click **Edit** to display the Ribbon as shown below.

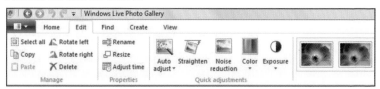

Display the group of pictures you want, either in the **Pictures Library** or in a folder of your choice on the hard disc drive.

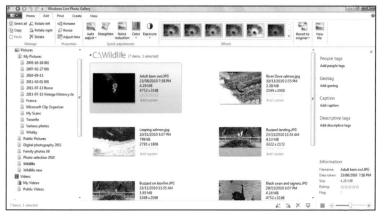

In the view of the Photo Gallery shown above, all of the photos are displayed as icons or thumbnails. You can use the scroll wheel on a mouse or the scroll bar at the right-hand side of the main panel to scroll through all of the images. To begin editing an image, use a single click to select it so that it's highlighted in blue as shown above. You can change the size of the icons or thumbnails by dragging the small slider at the bottom right of the screen and shown here on the right.

In this example, the icons or thumbnails are displayed after selecting **All details** on the **View** tab, as described in the previous chapter, page 74.

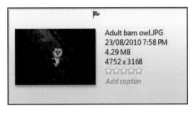

### Editing Photo Information

This information about each photo can be edited in the **Tag and caption** pane on the right of the screen when the **Edit** tab is selected, as shown on the right. You can also add a **Caption** and various tags as discussed in Chapter 10. The file size cannot be changed here but you can edit the name, give a star rating and flag the image. Later you may wish to filter out just the photos you have flagged during a search using the Photo Gallery **Find** tab.

### Viewing a Single Photo When Using the Edit Tab

The main screenshot on the previous page displays all of the photos in a folder as icons or thumbnails. To edit a particular photograph you need to view it full size on its own as shown on page 79. A quick way to view a single photo is to double-click anywhere on the icon or thumbnail of the photo.

With a single image displayed in the Photo Gallery, you can zoom in and out using the slider at the bottom of the screen, as shown at the bottom right and on the previous page.

You can change to display a different single image using the **Forward** and **Back** arrow buttons shown on the left below.

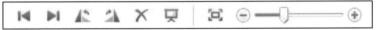

Alternate between single image view and multiple thumbnails view by double-clicking over the image or over a thumbnail.

# The Editing Tools

Several important basic editing tools appear in the centre of the Ribbon with the **Edit** tab selected, as shown below.

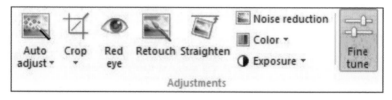

## Auto Adjust

This tool changes several properties of an image with just a single click. These include straightening, colour and exposure. The **Edit** settings can be switched on or off after clicking the small arrow next to **Auto adjust** and then selecting **Settings....**

Dragging the slider shown above allows you to control the quality and size of the image's JPEG file on the hard disc drive — high quality and a large file versus low quality and a small file size.

## The Crop Tool

The photograph of a Barn Owl shown in thumbnail form in the Windows Explorer on the right was taken at dusk, from quite a long way off. This is the original image copied from the camera to the hard disc drive, with no editing as yet. The file

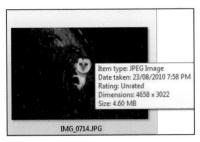

name **IMG_0714.JPG** was assigned automatically by the camera. If you allow the cursor to hover over the thumbnail in the Windows Explorer, basic information about the image is displayed as shown above on the right. This includes the date and time taken, the resolution and the file size.

Cropping should allow the surplus foliage to be removed enabling the owl itself to be enlarged. Modern 14 megapixel cameras enable an image to be considerably enlarged with no apparent loss of quality, except perhaps to the most discerning professional photographer. (4658 x 3022 pixels above equates to 14MP). Resolution and pixels are discussed in Chapters 2 and 8.

Open the Windows Live Photo Gallery and double-click the thumbnail of the required image. The full size image opens on the screen ready for editing, as shown below.

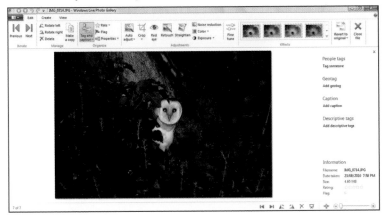

Select the **Edit** tab on the Ribbon and then click the **Crop** icon near the centre of the tab, as shown on the right. A grid of squares appears in the centre of the screen as shown below. This is the crop rectangle

which can be adjusted to enclose only the required part of the image.

The crop area is adjusted using the small squares which appear in each corner and in the middle of each side. Allow the cursor to hover over a square until a small two-headed arrow appears. Drag this arrow to frame the image at the required size. (The four -headed arrow which may also appear simply moves the entire crop frame around the image).

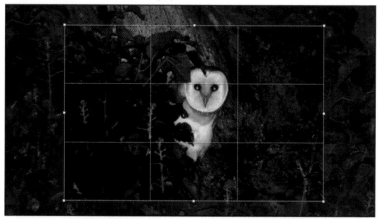

To set the cropped area at the same proportions as standard photographs, click the arrow beneath the **Crop** icon and choose **Proportion** and a size such as **5x7** shown on the right. Finally click **Apply crop** to complete the operation as shown on the right. The cropped owl photograph is shown on the next page.

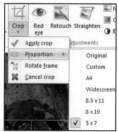

The cropped image is displayed filling the entire Photo Gallery window and this display size is controlled by the Taskbar icon shown on the right and below.

Clicking the above icon, (which changes after clicking) alternates the display between the image's actual size and a size which just fits inside the Photo Gallery window, as shown above at the top.

In this example the effect of cropping is to reduce the size of the image file from 4.6MB to 1.14MB. The new size also appears in the **Tag and caption pane** on the right of the screen.

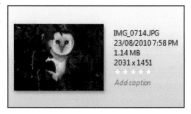

IMG_0714.JPG
23/08/2010 7:58 PM
1.14 MB
2031 x 1451
*Add caption*

### Undoing Editing Changes

If you don't like the result of an editing operation such as cropping, click **Revert to original** on the right of the Ribbon with the **Edit** tab selected, to undo the changes you've just made.

Revert to original ▾

## Removing Red Eye

The image of the owl was viewed at actual size by clicking on the Taskbar icon as discussed on the previous page. This produced a very much bigger image which could be scrolled by dragging with the mouse. As shown below, the image appeared to have a touch of "red eye".

Red eye is a photographic effect which occurs when using flash photography. Windows Live Photo Gallery has a **Red eye** tool launched from an icon near the centre of the Ribbon, with the **Edit** tab selected. When you click the **Red eye** icon a small cross appears allowing you to draw a white frame round an affected eye. After applying the **Red eye** tool, the owl's eye changed to blue as shown in the lower image on the right.

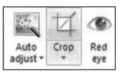

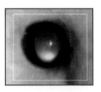

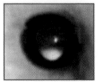

You can also undo any unwanted editing changes if you click the **Undo** icon at the top left-hand corner of the screen. However, this must be done straightaway.

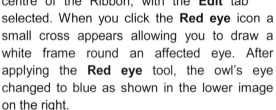

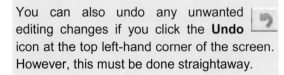

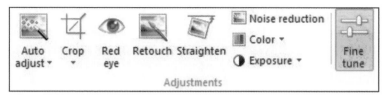

**Retouch** shown on the **Edit** tab above allows you to drag a rectangle around an area of a photo to remove blemishes and imperfections. A single click of the **Straighten** button aligns the image horizontally, if necessary. There are also buttons on the left-hand side of the **Edit** tab to rotate the image through 90 degrees left and right. These might be used say, if you had turned your camera vertically to take a photograph.

The **Noise reduction**, **Color** and **Exposure** shown above all make changes automatically if you just click the icon. Noise is unwanted coloured speckles. If you click the arrows next to **Color** or **Exposure**, a grid showing different settings is displayed, allowing you to experiment and select one, if it's an improvement. The available settings for **Exposure** are shown on the right. The **Color** (colour) adjustment works in a similar way.

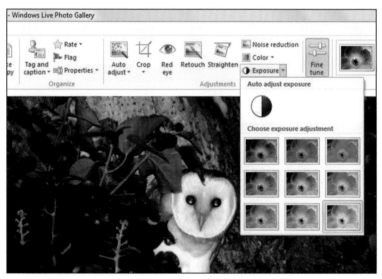

**Manual Editing with Fine Tune**

Many users will probably find the single-click editing tools such as **Auto adjust** are perfectly capable of improving their images to a very satisfactory standard. However, if you want to polish your images by applying each effect manually, the Windows Live Photo Gallery has several precision tools to help you achieve the desired effects.

Click **Fine tune** on the Ribbon, as shown on the right and on the previous page. The right-hand panel on the screen changes from displaying the **Tag and caption pane** to display the following list of editing tasks.

When you click any of the four editing tasks listed on the right, one or more sliders appear, as shown below on the right with 4 sliders for **Adjust exposure**. Drag a slider with the mouse until you achieve the desired effect. You can use the undo icon shown on the right to remove any unwanted effects or click **Revert to original** on the Ribbon as described earlier.

Adjust exposure

Adjust color

Straighten photo

Adjust detail

### The Effects Group

The group of icons shown below appear on the right-hand side of the Ribbon with the **Edit** tab selected.

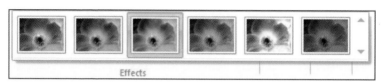

Clicking any of the above icons changes the entire colour scheme of the selected photo. The available effects are black and white, sepia tone, cyan tone and orange, yellow and red filters.

## The End Result

The images below show the owl and a buzzard before and after editing in the Windows Live Photo Gallery, using the crop and red eye removal tools and the automatic adjustment buttons mentioned earlier.

**A Barn Owl On Its Nest**

**A Buzzard Landing On A Bonfire**

# Making a Copy of a Photograph

Whenever you edit a photograph in the Photo Gallery, the changes are saved automatically. The Photo Gallery also keeps a copy of the original photo before it was edited in a folder called **Original Images**. However, you might want to keep several versions of a photograph. This can be done using **Make a copy** from the Photo Gallery Ribbon with the **Edit** tab selected, as shown below.

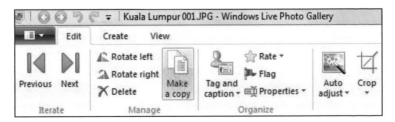

The **Make a copy** window opens, as shown in the extract below.

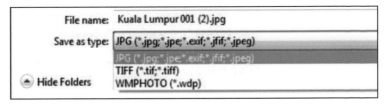

You can enter a new name in the **File name** slot shown above, otherwise the existing file name will be used but with a suffix such as (2) or (3) for example.

### Photographs Saved as TIFF Files

By default the new version of a file will be saved in the popular JPEG or .jpg format but you can also use the TIFF (Tagged Image File Format) as shown above. TIFF files are used in applications where high quality images are required, but occupy much more space on the hard disc drive. While a JPEG file might have a typical file size of 3MB, the TIFF version of the same photograph could easily be 16MB.

# 8

# Further Editing of Photographs

## Introduction

The previous chapter described some of the most common photo editing tasks, aimed at improving and polishing an image. This chapter takes a look at some of the additional editing facilities provided by the Windows Live Photo Gallery, such as:

- Adding Ratings, Flags and Tags to photographs displayed in the Windows Live Photo Gallery. This makes groups of photos easy to find and display.

- Adding captions to thumbnails using the Windows Live Photo Gallery.

- Resizing a picture so that it uses less disc storage space and can be e-mailed or posted to a Web site quickly.

- Creating a panoramic view by stitching together two or more images of the same scene.

- Adding captions to full size photos and slide shows using the Windows Paint program.

This chapter also includes some further discussion of image resolution as mentioned in Chapter 2. This concerns the number of pixels or dots in a photograph and limits the maximum size of a print on paper. Above a certain size the actual pixels become visible to the naked eye; this is known as pixellation. High resolution images can be printed satisfactorily at a larger paper size than images of lower resolution.

# Further Editing Features

The **Iterate**, **Manage** and **Organize** groups of icons shown below appear on the Photo Gallery Ribbon when you have the **Edit** tab selected and you are viewing a single photograph on the full screen. The **Edit** ribbon is different when viewing multiple icons or thumbnails in the Photo Gallery.

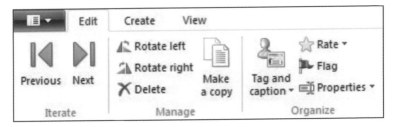

The above **Iterate** arrows allow you to move through the images in the current folder, displaying them full size one at a time.

The panel on the right-hand side of the screen, shown here on the right, lists any tags and captions which have been set on a selected photo.

The **Tag and caption** icon shown on the Ribbon above switches this right-hand panel on and off.

**Rate** shown on the Ribbon above allows you to attach a star rating from 0-5 to the current image. **Flag** attaches a small flag to the image and this appears on the thumbnail of the image. The flag is also displayed in red in the **Tag and caption** panel in the **Information** section shown on the right. Flagging a number of images enables you to

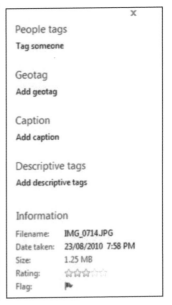

filter them out later, using the **Find** tab as discussed earlier.

## Captions

If you click **Add caption** shown in the **Tag and caption** panel  at the bottom right of the previous page, you can enter a title or a few descriptive words such as **Salmon at Norbury**, shown below. The image has also been flagged and given a 5-star rating.

Please note that the captions only appear on the thumbnails of the photos in the Photo Gallery. They do not appear on the full size photos, for example when displaying them in a slide show. However, captions can easily be added to full size photographs using Windows Paint, a program included as part of all recent versions of Microsoft Windows and this is discussed shortly.

Captions, flags, tags and ratings can be used to search for and display certain groups of images using the **Find** tab discussed earlier. Tags are discussed in more detail in Chapter 10.

The **Properties** icon shown on the Ribbon on the previous page opens the small menu shown on the right. **Rename** allows you to change the file name of a photo. For example, the original name such as **IMG_0714.JPG** under **Information** at the bottom of the previous image could be replaced with something more meaningful, such as **Adult Barn Owl**. **Adjust time** allows you to change the time displayed under **Information** shown at the bottom of the previous page.

## Resizing an Image

An image file can be made smaller to make it quicker to e-mail or post to a Web site. The resized image file will also take up less space on a storage medium such as a hard disc drive.

The size of a photo here refers to the resolution or number of pixels in the image. In the example on the right, the camera was set at 14MP (megapixels) or 4288 pixels wide by 3216 pixels

high. It's a good idea to take photos at the highest resolution setting on your camera. This is because it's easier to reduce the number of pixels in an image than to increase them. This *resampling downwards* involves discarding pixels. *Resampling upwards* (inserting pixels that have been artificially created by the software) is also possible but may not produce perfect results.

The size of a particular image can be thought of as a finite number of pixels. This fixed number of  pixels can be stretched or squashed as different sized pictures depending on the medium, whether it's a computer monitor, or a print on a specified size of paper such as 5"x7" or 8"x10". Programs such as the Windows Live Photo Gallery usually display the image to fit the program's screen window. There is also an option to display the image at its actual size, which may be much too large to fit on the screen.

With the required image displayed full size in the Photo Gallery, select **Properties** from the Ribbon with the **Edit** tab selected, as shown on page 88. Then select **Resize** from the drop-down menu as shown on the

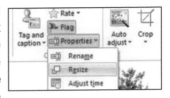

right. The **Resize** window opens with a drop-down menu offering a range of pixel widths from **1280** down to **640** and also a **Custom** option, as shown on the next page.

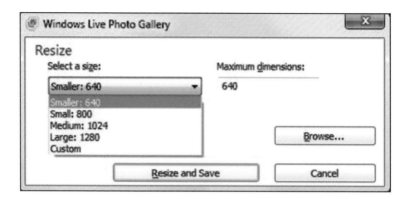

After selecting a pixel width such as **640**, click **Resize and Save** as shown above. The smaller image is saved with the new resolution **(640x480)** appended to the file name. The original full size image is

preserved on the hard disc. The original image had a file size of 4.63MB, sixteen times greater than the 285KB of the 640x480 image. The quality of the smaller image compared well with the original image when displayed full size on the screen in the Photo Gallery window. However, when printed on paper at A4 size, the pixels were clearly visible in the 640x480 image.

**Key Points: Image Size**

- Higher resolution images make better prints at a higher paper size than prints made from low resolution images.

- Resize an image downwards by discarding pixels in a program such as Windows Live Photo gallery.

- The smaller image will be quicker to send by e-mail or post to a Web site, and occupy less disc storage space.

- Image size can also be reduced by cropping.

- Keep a copy of the original, full size, unedited image.

## Pixellation

This refers to the appearance of the small coloured squares or pixels (picture elements) which make up an image. The following photograph had been resized down to a resolution of 640x480 pixels. Even though this is a low resolution image, to the casual observer the image is not obviously pixellated on the screen.

However, when a low resolution image is enlarged or stretched the pixellation becomes obvious, as shown by the signet's head on the left, after stretching the image in the Windows Paint program. (Paint is discussed shortly).

**As a rough guide, when printing on paper at 300 pixels per inch or 300 dots per inch:**

**A 3MP image has a maximum print size of 7"x5".**

**A 14MP image has a maximum print size of 15"x10".**

**(MP is short for megapixels or millions of pixels).**

# Creating a Panoramic View

Sometimes a single camera shot will not do justice to a wide landscape. The Panorama feature in the Windows Live Photo Gallery allows you to take two or more separate photos of the same scene and "stitch" them together to make a single image. Ideally the separate images will cover different parts of the landscape but will have a degree of overlap. By matching up the common features in the overlapped area the program is able to make a seamless join.

First select the required images in the Photo Gallery, by holding down the **Ctrl** key while clicking the images. The selected images are highlighted in blue, as shown below.

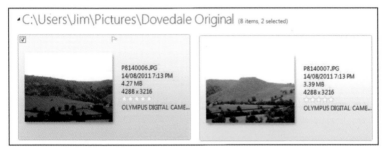

Now click the **Create** tab on the Ribbon and click the **Panorama** icon as shown  below. The stitching process then begins.

The **Stitching panorama photo** window opens with a bar indicating progress, which can take a few minutes.

At the end of the stitching process the **Save** window appears. By default the new panoramic image takes the name of one of the original images but with **Stitch** added as in **P8140007 Stitch.jpg**. If you prefer you can enter a different **File name**.

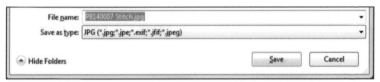

The new panoramic view appears, as shown below. You may need to use the **Crop** tool to trim up the edges of the new composite image. Cropping  was discussed in the last chapter.

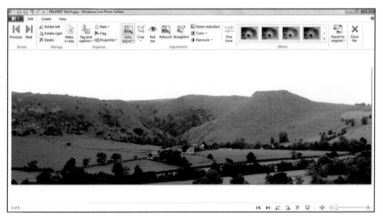

In thumbnail view, the panoramic image (**P8140007 Stitch.jpg** in the centre below) is saved alongside the thumbnails of the original images used to make the panorama.

# Using Windows Paint to Add Captions

## Introducing Paint

As discussed earlier in this chapter, the Windows Live Photo Gallery allows you to add captions, i.e. a few words of information about an image. However, captions added in this way only appear on the thumbnails in the Photo Gallery and in the **Tag and caption pane** on the right of the screen. These captions do not appear on the images when they are displayed full size in a slide show or when photos are printed on paper. Such captions are helpful when showing other people your photos. Fortunately all recent versions of Microsoft Windows include the **Paint** drawing and painting program, launched after clicking the **Start** button and selecting **All Programs**, **Accessories** and **Paint**. Paint has a Ribbon containing a full range of drawing tools including **Crop**, **Resize**, **Rotate**, ready made shapes and you can draw and fill using a large palette.

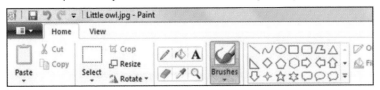

Paint can be used to edit photographs with the drawing and text tools and in particular to add captions as discussed on the next page. There is also a **Save as** option on the **File** menu which allows you to resave photos in different formats such as **GIF**, giving a small file size for images used in e-mails or on the Web.

Digressing slightly, the screenshots in this book are made using Paint. First the screen is copied to an area of memory known as the Clipboard, by pressing the Print Screen (Prt Sc) key. Then the screen image is pasted into Paint where it can be cropped and edited. Finally the required area is selected and then copied and pasted into the text of the book in Microsoft Publisher.

**Copy** and **Paste** icons appear on the Paint Ribbon and on a menu when you right-click over an object on the screen.

## Adding a Caption Using Windows Paint

Open the Windows Live Photo Gallery and right-click over the thumbnail for the required photograph. From the menu which pops up select **Open with** and then click **Paint** from the next menu. The photograph opens in Paint as shown below.

Select the text icon **A** on the Paint Ribbon and draw a suitable text box. Then select the font size and colours for the text (**Color 1**) and background (**Color 2**) as shown on the Ribbon below. Enter the text of the caption.

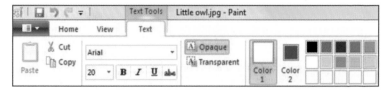

Click the disc icon at the top left-hand corner of the screen to save the photo together with the new caption. The caption will now appear when the photo appears full size and in slide shows.

# Printing and Sharing Photographs

## Introduction

When you've finished polishing and editing your photos, you'll probably want to show them to other people. With computers and digital photography there are numerous ways to share your pictures. Some of these methods were just not possible in the era of the film-based camera. A few of the most popular ways of sharing digital photographs are as follows:

- Making your own prints at home to show to friends and relatives, using an inkjet or laser printer and special high quality photo paper.

- Taking your memory card or other media containing your photographs to make prints at one of the High Street photo printing services.

- Using an online printing service to make prints and also incorporate your photos into calendars and mugs, etc. These will usually be delivered by traditional post.

- Including your photographs with e-mails to friends and family wherever they are in the world.

- Posting photos to a social networking Web site such as Facebook or a photo-sharing Web site like Flickr. Then your photos can be viewed by anyone who has your permission and a connection to the World Wide Web.

- Illustrating a talk to a club or society by presenting your photographs in a slide show using a projector attached to a laptop computer.

# Printing a Photograph

Unless you're just making a quick draft print, use special photo quality paper in the printer. This is available from many High Street stores although it can be expensive so it's worth shopping around. Open the required photograph in the Windows Live Photo Gallery and display the drop-down **File** menu by clicking the icon shown on the right, located in the top left-hand corner of the screen. Then click the **Print** option in the **File** menu in the left-hand panel as shown below.

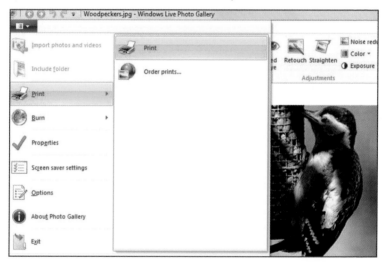

Clicking **Order prints...** shown above takes you directly to a list of available online photo printing companies. Online printing services are discussed shortly.

Click **Print** as shown in the centre panel above to open the **Print Pictures** window shown on the next page. This has drop-down menus enabling you to select a different printer, (if available), and to set the paper size and type of paper compatible with what is actually in your printer. There is also an option to set the print quality ranging from **Fast Draft**, through **Normal**, **Best** to **Maximum dpi**.

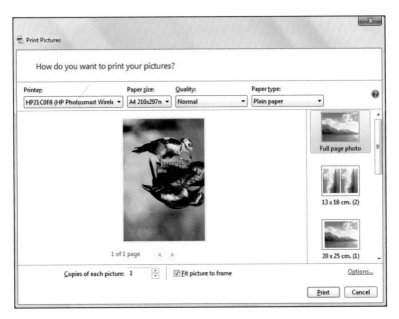

As can be seen in the panel on the right above, you can choose the number of photos per page. If you have several pictures selected in a group or folder in the Windows Live Photo Gallery or the Windows Explorer (discussed in detail in Chapter 10), they will all be printed in sequence in whatever layout you have chosen, such as two or four per page (as shown in the print preview panel on the right). You can select multiple copies of each picture. There is also an **Options** link which allows you to alter many of the settings on your printer such as fast and economical printing. Finally click the **Print** button to start the printing process.

# Photo Printing Services

There are many large photo printing companies who can reproduce your digital photographs very quickly to a high standard. If you're printing lots of photos it can be very slow on a cheap inkjet printer at home. A typical price for a 7"x 5" print might be 10p but may be nearer 5p for larger numbers of prints.

### High Street Printing

Enter something like **photo printing stores** into a search program like Google or Bing and you will find numerous companies such as Jessops and Boots with a High Street presence and stores across the UK.

---

Photo Prints Offers - 7x5 - Print for the Price of 6x4. ⌕
www.jessops.com/Photo-Prints-Offers - jessops.com is rated ★★★★⯪  1,375 reviews
Free Delivery to Store. Ends 24Aug.
7x5 Prints on Price of 6x4 - Buy 1 Get 1 Half Price Photobooks - 30% Off Calendars

Boots Photo Prints | Bootsphoto.com ⌕
www.bootsphoto.com/50-Free-Prints
50 Free Prints when you Join Boots Photo & earn advantage card points.

---

Then select **Store Locator** to find a branch near where you live. Some stores may do the printing for you while you wait and others, such as Max Spielmann, for example, have self-service machines into which you insert the camera's memory card containing your images. Touch screen technology allows you to select which photos to print. Alternatively, if you've transferred your images and edited them on your computer, you might copy them onto a CD, DVD or flash drive (also known as a memory stick). The photo print store will be able to print photos from these alternative storage media instead of the camera's memory card.

Images on a mobile phone may also be printed either from the phone's memory card or using Bluetooth, a type of short range wireless technology available on some mobile phones.

Some standalone, self-service printing machines are available in public areas such as shopping precincts, providing instant prints.

## Online Printing Services

Companies offering online printing of photographs provide the necessary free software for you to select the required photographs and upload them to the Internet for printing at the company's premises.

The finished prints are normally posted back to you within a few days. Jessops offer a service in which you can order prints online but collect them from your nearest Jessops' store, instead of having them posted to your home address. This might save up to £15 in postage.

Some companies, such as Vistaprint, allow you to upload your photos and have them printed on items such as calendars, mouse mats, mugs and greetings cards. An extract from a calendar we produced from photographs we uploaded to the Vistaprint Web site (**www.vistaprint.co.uk**) is shown below.

# Sending Photographs With an E-mail

You can send your photos in a special *photo e-mail* or as *attachments* i.e. files added or "clipped" to an e-mail message.

## Sending a Photo E-mail

To send a photo e-mail you need to have the Windows Live Mail program on your computer. This free software is part of Windows Live Essentials and downloaded in the same way as Windows Live Photo Gallery, as described on page 10.

Open the Photo Gallery as previously described or by clicking **Start**, **All Programs** and **Windows Live Photo Gallery**. Select and highlight the photographs you want to send by clicking with the mouse while simultaneously holding down the **Ctrl** key.

## SkyDrive Photo Hosting

With the **Home** tab selected in the Photo Gallery, click the small arrow next to **Photo email** and select **Send photo email**, as shown above. The Windows Live Mail program opens as shown on the right, with your photographs already inserted on the page. Enter the text of the message
and the address of the recipient and click the **Send** button. In a **Photo email** the images are sent to SkyDrive, an online Microsoft file hosting service. The recipient of a **Photo email** can view a slide show of the photos or download them to their computer. They do not need to be sent a link or the permission normally required to access someone's SkyDrive files.

## Sending Photographs as E-mail Attachments

With the photographs selected in the Photo Gallery as previously described, click **Send photos as attachments** from the drop-down **Photo email** menu as shown on the previous page. The window shown on the right appears, allowing you to reduce your images to a size suitable for e-mailing as attachments. The **Medium** setting shown on the right should be okay for most purposes.

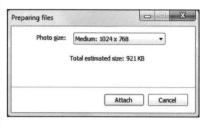

When you click **Attach**, as shown above, your default e-mail program opens with the photos already attached as shown by the three **Rome** photo files below.

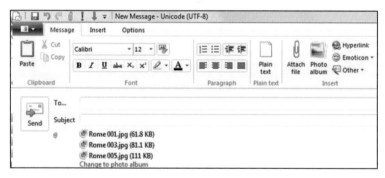

Enter the recipient's details and the e-mail text, then click **Send**. The recipient can click options to view the photos as a slide show or download them and save them as files on their computer.

# Posting Photographs to a Web Site

The Windows Live Photo Gallery makes it easy for you to upload photos to various Web sites so that other people can view them wherever they are in the world. Icons for some of the main photo sharing Web sites appear on the Photo Gallery Ribbon, as shown below in the **Share** group with the **Home** tab selected.

SkyDrive is Microsoft's own file storage site on the Internet somewhere in the "clouds", enabling you to upload and share thousands of files, including photos. The photos can be viewed by your friends via e-mails or by links set up in SkyDrive and sent to social networks such as Facebook.

Facebook is the world's largest social network with over 750 million users. You can control who sees your photos, news and personal information in Facebook.

YouTube shown above on the Photo Gallery Ribbon is a site for uploading videos and sharing them with other people.

The icon shown on the right and on the Ribbon above represents Flickr, a Web site primarily dedicated to the management and sharing of photographs.

The following is a general method for uploading photos:

- In the Photo Gallery, select the photos to be uploaded.
- On the **Home** tab **Share** group, select the required service such as Facebook. Follow the instructions on the screen to upload the images.
- This topic is covered in more detail in my book **Facebook for the Older Generation (BP 723)** from Bernard Babani (publishing) Ltd.

# Managing Photos in Windows Explorer

## Introduction

The Windows Explorer is the main file handling program within the Microsoft Windows operating system. The Windows Explorer is used frequently, so its icon (shown on the right) is permanently pinned to the Taskbar at the bottom of the screen. The Windows Explorer is not to be confused with the Internet Explorer, the Web browser launched by clicking the icon shown on the right. Both icons are also shown below pinned to the Windows Taskbar.

The Windows Explorer has many useful functions, such as:

- Showing the available resources on your computer including the hard disc drive, CD/DVD drive and any removable storage devices attached such as a camera.

- Displaying the various libraries and folders containing files of different types including digital photographs.

- Displaying files as icons in a range of sizes and giving details and properties of files, including photographs.

- Creating hierarchies of folders and sub-folders enabling photo files to be organised in a meaningful structure.

- Carrying out file management tasks such as copying, moving, renaming and deleting files and folders.

- Searching for photos stored on your computer including the use of tags to identify particular groups of images.

- Making backup copies of photos onto a CD for security.

# The Windows Explorer

Earlier chapters showed how the Windows Live Photo Gallery makes it simple to import photos into your computer then organise and edit them. Whereas the Photo Gallery is dedicated to working with photographs, the Windows Explorer is capable of managing all types of file such as text documents, in addition to photographs. A good knowledge of the Windows Explorer is essential for managing your computer's saved files and folders efficiently, including your libraries of photographs.

The Windows Explorer is launched by clicking the Taskbar icon shown on the right. Then click **Computer** shown in the left-hand panel. Alternatively click the Start button and select **Compute**r from the Start menu. (In Windows XP select **My Computer** from the Start menu.)

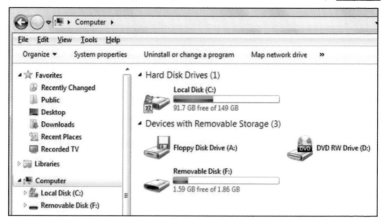

**Local Disk (C:)** above is the main fixed hard disc drive inside the computer, used for storing all your programs and data, such as photographs. **Floppy Disk Drive (A:)** is virtually obsolete as this medium has been replaced by CDs/DVDs and flash drives. The drive labelled **DVD RW Drive (D:)** can save photos on both CDs and DVDs and is useful for making secure backup copies of important photographs, as discussed shortly.

## Displaying a Memory Card in the Windows Explorer

When you connect your camera's memory card to a computer as described in Chapter 3, it shows up as another disc drive. In this example, the memory card has been connected using a card reader and has been labelled automatically as **Removable**

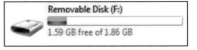

**Disk (F:)**. The Windows Explorer also shows that there is **1.59 GB** of free space available for more photos on the memory card.

After you connect a storage device like the camera's memory card, it is also listed in the left-hand panel of the Windows Explorer, shown here under **Computer** as **Removable Disk (F:)**.

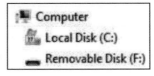

## Examining the Photos on the Memory Card

Double-click the camera card, **Removable Disk (F:)** in this example, then double-click the folders on the card until you find the images you want. As shown below, the images of Rome were in the main folder **DCIM** and sub-folder **100OLYMP**, as created by the digital camera.

The full path name through the folders on the memory card, **Removable Disk (F:)**, is therefore:

## Transferring Photos Using the Windows Explorer

This section shows how you can copy photographs direct from your camera's memory card to your computer's hard disc drive. This is an alternative method to those described in Chapter 4, which import your photos automatically to the **Pictures Library**.

Shortly the creation of your own hierarchy of folders is discussed. The following method uses the simple Windows **Copy** and **Paste** commands to transfer your photos to a folder of your choice on the hard disc. Creating your own folders is discussed shortly.

### Selecting the Images

Display the folder containing the images in the Windows Explorer as just described. If necessary select **View** from the menu bar and choose a suitable size for the images such as **Large icons**. Then select the photos you want to copy by keeping the **Ctrl** key held down while clicking the required images. The images to be copied should appear highlighted against a blue background.

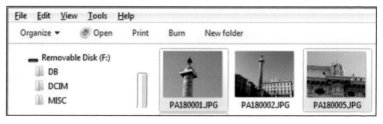

### Copying the Images to the Clipboard

Now right-click over any one of the highlighted images and select (using a left-click this time) the **Copy** option from the menu which pops up. Alternatively select **Edit** from the menu bar and click **Copy** from the drop-down menu. This copies the photos to a temporary memory storage area known as the *clipboard*. The **Cut** command on the two previously mentioned menus would place copies of the images on the clipboard but would remove them from the original source, i.e. the memory card.

## Pasting the Photos to a Folder on the Hard Disc Drive

With the images copied to the clipboard, they can now be pasted to any folder on the hard disc drive **(C:)**. In the example below the destination folder **Holiday 2011** has been selected by a single click in the left-hand panel of the Windows Explorer under **Local Disk (C:)**. Now right-click over this destination folder and select **Paste** from the menu which pops up. Alternatively click **Edit** on the menu bar and select **Paste** from the drop-down menu. The photos now appear in the destination folder **Holiday 2011** as shown below.

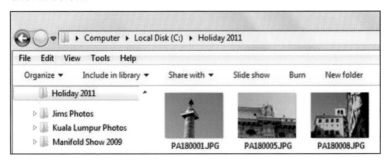

Now the photographs can be managed in the Windows Explorer as discussed shortly.

## Creating Your Own Folders

If you want to make your own system of folders, select the drive such as the **(C:)** drive. Then click **New folder** from the menu bar shown below.

Next type the name of the folder in the slot, replacing the words **New folder**. The new folder will then be listed in the left-hand panel of the Windows Explorer under the **(C:) drive.**

## Creating a Hierarchy of Folders and Sub-folders

You can create a *sub-folder* within an existing folder by first selecting the existing folder in the Windows Explorer. Then select **New folder** from the menu bar as described on the previous page. Then enter the name of the sub-folder. This process can continue, creating sub-folders within sub-folders until you have a tree or hierarchical structure of folders and sub-folders. In the example below, a folder called **Holidays** has been created on the (**C:**) drive. Then a sub-folder **France** was created within **Holidays** and then a sub-folder **Nice** within **France**.

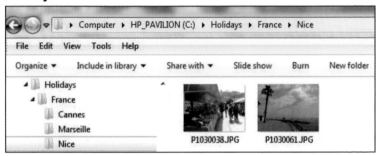

## Dragging and Dropping Files Such As Photos

You can use drag and drop with the mouse to move or copy files such as photos from one folder to another. Select the required images in the Windows Explorer then hover over one of them and, keeping the left mouse button held down, drag the images and drop them into the destination folder by releasing the mouse button. If the images are dragged to a folder on the same disc drive, they are *moved.* If the images are dragged to a folder on a different disc drive they are *copied*, leaving the original images in place. If you drag with the *right* button held down, on releasing the mouse button, a menu appears allowing you to select either **Copy here** or **Move here**. This method can be used to import photos from your camera's memory card to your hard disc drive or (**C:**) drive.

Copy here

**Move here**

Create shortcuts here

Cancel

## Useful Tasks

Click **View** in the Windows Explorer and choose from a range of sizes for the icons or thumbnails. Select **Details** to display the photo files with the information shown below. Click the title at the top of a column to sort them into a particular order such as date.

| Name | Date | Type | Size | Tags |
|------|------|------|------|------|
| P1030038.JPG | 22/06/2011 9:02 AM | JPEG Image | 3,427 KB | |
| P1030061.JPG | 23/06/2011 11:15 AM | JPEG Image | 2,780 KB | |

When you right-click over the thumbnail or name of a photo file in the Windows Explorer, the menu shown on the right appears, containing many useful options. For example, **Print** opens the **Print Pictures** window as shown on page 99. **Edit** opens the photograph in the Windows Paint program discussed earlier. **Open with** offers a choice of several progams to open the photograph in, such as Windows Live Photo Gallery and the Windows Photo Viewer. **Send to** copies the image to a range of destinations such as e-mail, CD/DVD, and any removable discs. **Cut** and **Copy** are discussed on page 108. **Delete** removes the photo

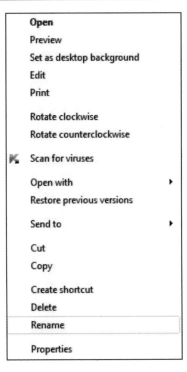

and places it in the **Recycle Bin**. **Rename** allows you to overwrite the file name from the camera, such as **P1030038.JPG** and replace it with a more meaningful name. **Properties** displays extensive details about a photograph.

Double-click an icon in the Windows Explorer to open a photograph in its default program, as discussed on page 55.

## Making Secure Backup Copies of Photographs

Precious photos stored on a hard disc drive can be accidentally deleted or lost, e.g. when a laptop is stolen. A safe way to make backup copies is to "burn" them onto a CD-R or DVD-R disc.

### Copying Photos to a CD-R or DVD-R

- Select the required photos in the Windows Explorer as previously described, holding down the **Ctrl** key while clicking with the mouse to select multiple photos.
- Select **Burn** from the Windows Explorer menu bar.
- When requested insert a writeable CD/DVD in the drive.
- Click **Next** and then select **With a CD/DVD player.**
- Click **Next** and select **Burn to Disc** from the menu bar.

The blank disc is then prepared and the photographs are copied as shown below in the **Burn to Disc** window.

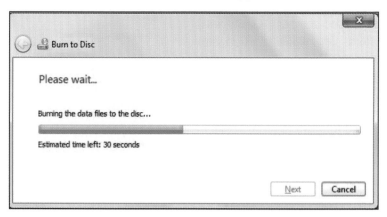

At the end of the process you are given the chance to copy the same photos to another CD/DVD or to click **Finish**. It's a good idea to label the CDs or DVDs and keep them in a safe place.

## Tagged Images

A tag can be just a name added to certain photographs with something in common. For example, when photographs of Rome were imported, they were tagged as shown on page 38. To find those pictures amongst the many thousands on the hard disc drive **(C:)**, open the Windows Explorer using the icon on the Task bar shown on the  right. Click the **(C:)** drive then type the tag name into the Search bar at the top right of the Windows Explorer screen. Or select the tag if it already appears in the drop-down menu  when you click the Search bar. After selecting or entering **Rome** all the pictures tagged **Rome** are displayed. In this example, 68 photos were found and displayed instantly out of 2051 images on the hard disc drive.

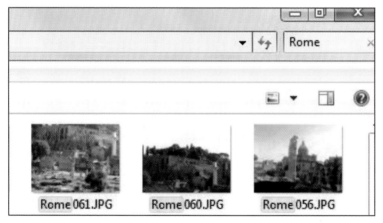

In the drop-down menu above, selecting **\*.jpg**, will find and display all of the photos on your hard disc which have the popular **.jpg** file name extension (also known as the **JPEG** file type) used by most digital cameras.

**Adding a Tag**

Open the Windows Explorer by clicking the Taskbar icon shown on the right. Open the folder containing the photos you want to tag, such as the **Pictures Library**  or a folder you have created on the hard disc drive. Use a single click to select the icon or thumbnail for the photo to be tagged. The selected photograph should now appear against a blue background. To select multiple photos, hold down the **Ctrl** key while continuing to click (single click) the photos to be tagged.

At the bottom of the screen you should see the **Details** pane giving information about the selected image(s). If you can't see the **Details** pane, in the Windows Explorer, select **Organize** from the menu bar, then click **Layout** and then **Details pane**.

Type in the name of the tag, such as **Our cat Bop** replacing the words **Add a tag**, as shown above and below.

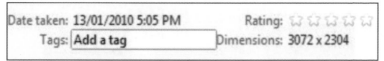

Click **Save** on the right-hand side and the tag can now be used in the Search bar of the Windows Explorer and in the **Find** tab in the Photo Gallery to quickly find the tagged images from all those on your hard disc. As shown above, you can also give an image a star **Rating**, to be used in filtering out your best or worst images using the **Find** tab in the Windows Live Photo Gallery.

# Appendix: Notes for Users of Windows XP

This book was produced using a PC computer running the Windows 7 operating system. It is recognised that many people are still using the earlier versions of the operating system, namely Windows Vista and Windows XP.

The material in this book should be completely compatible with machines running Windows Vista. The general methods in this book are also compatible in principle with Windows XP but there are some differences in details such as screen layouts. For example, Windows XP uses the  rectangular **Start** button shown on the right compared with the spherical button in Windows 7.

In Windows XP the Windows Explorer program used for managing files including photos is launched from the **Start** menu while in Windows 7 there is also an icon, shown on the right, permanently pinned to the Taskbar. Like Windows 7, the Windows Explorer in Windows XP has all the options for copying, pasting, deleting and renaming photos as described in this book. There are also options to send photos with e-mails, copy to a CD or publish to the Web.

In addition Window XP uses slightly different versions of the Windows Paint and Photo Gallery programs described in this book. Whereas Windows 7 uses the latest tabbed Ribbon in the Paint program, Windows XP uses the more traditional menu with **File**, **Edit** and **View**, etc., as shown below.

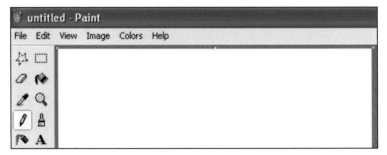

## Windows Live Photo Gallery for Windows XP

The Photo Gallery is referred to throughout the text; Windows 7 and Vista use the same version of the Photo Gallery but Windows XP uses a slightly different edition. Both versions can be downloaded from the Web site **http://explore.live.com** as described on page 10 of this book. However, users of Windows XP should click **Essentials**, **Photo Gallery**, **Learn about Photo Gallery for Windows XP** before following the instructions to download the version of the software for their machine.

The general procedures for importing photos to the Photo Gallery in Windows XP are the same as described in this book. The Photo Gallery in XP uses a menu bar containing **File**, **Fix**, **Info**, etc., as shown below, rather than the Ribbon in the Windows 7 version. There is an **Auto adjust** button to improve images with a single click and further options to manually edit photos, correct exposure, straighten, crop and fix red eye, as shown below.

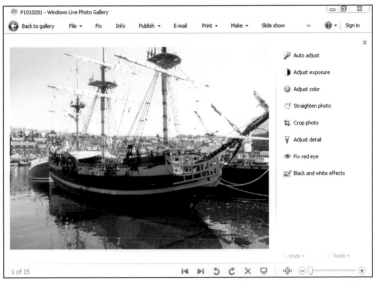

The Windows XP Photo Gallery also has options to publish photos on the Web, e-mail, print and display in a slide show.